PONS

Jetzt klappt's!
GERMAN Grammar

Learning grammar the easy way

by
Stefanie Plisch de Vega

Assisted by
Agnieszka Grzesiak

Ernst Klett Sprachen GmbH
Barcelona • Belgrad • Budapest • Ljubljana • London • Posen • Prag
Sofia • Stuttgart • Zagreb

PONS
Jetzt klappt's!
GERMAN Grammar

Learning grammar the easy way

by
Stefanie Plisch de Vega

Assisted by
Agnieszka Grzesiak

Auflage A1 5 4 3 2 1 / 2008 2007 2006 2005

Internet: www.pons.de
E-Mail: info@pons.de

Editor: Antje Wollenweber
Logo design: Erwin Poell, Heidelberg
Logo redesign: Sabine Redlin, Ludwigsburg
Cover design: deutschewerbeagentur
Original illustrations: Walter Uihlein, Altdorf
Black/white-Illustrations: Norberto Lombardi, Campana
Layout: **beluga**design, Stuttgart
Typesetting: Regina Krawatzki, Stuttgart
Print: Legoprint
Printed in Italy.

ISBN: 3-12-561213-6

Welcome to your German grammar course!

Interested in learning German grammar not only quickly, but also in an entertaining and motivating way? Interested in understanding grammar rules thorougly and being able to put them to use?
Then this course is ideal for you. Not only will you become familiar with the most important aspects of the German grammar, but modern and communicative methods will also give you intensive grammar practice opportunities. What's more, you will be able to use the German grammar properly in real-life situations.
In addition, you will acquire a solid foundation in vocabulary, communication and cultural knowledge while you work through your way through tasks and exercises. This grammar course has been designed to meet the needs of both beginning learners and those with previous experience. It also contains solutions and tips to enhance your self-study progress.

Set-up of the grammar course:
The course consists of 12 modules and 12 tests. Each module starts with a short introduction of the topics it covers, which is then followed by detailed explanations and an exercise section. The modules are each followed up by a test in which you can test your understanding of that particular module.
In addition, an **Audio CD** is included containing recordings for exercises and texts. This will help you to consolidate your pronunciation and communication skills as well as develop your listening comprehension skills. The numbering of exercises throughout the course will indicate where you are and help you to find answers in the appendix quickly.

The icons used in the course have the following meanings:

TR.01 You need the audio CD. The tracks will show you where to find the right listening texts.

You need a pen to write or copy something down.

You need a pen to mark, tick or link something.

You need a separate piece of paper to complete the task.

You should pay special attention here and read the following text carefully!

Gut zu wissen Note that **Sie**, when used as the formal form of *you*, always starts with a capital letter.	You will find useful and interesting information and tips about the German language and culture.
lesen – *to read* **nehmen** – *to take* **fahren** – *to go, to drive*	You will find words and phrases which are relevant to the task in the vocabulary box.
wohnen ich wohne du wohnst er / sie / es wohnt wir wohnen ihr wohnt sie / Sie wohnen	You will find relevant verb forms in this box.
§ 22 Present tense	You are asked to look up additional grammatical information.

Appendix

Here you will find the following contents:

Answer key To check your answers, use the answer key.

Grammar overview Here, the most important grammar points covered in the course are explained in more depth.

Glossary This is an alphabetical list of all the words used in the course including translations.

We hope that this course will make learning German an enjoyable and succesful experience!

1 TR.01

Hello! Let's have a look at some German verbs. Try to match the following verbs to the correct translation. You can also listen to these verbs on the CD.

1. wohnen	*a. to know*
2. arbeiten	*b. to talk*
3. kommen	*c. to come*
4. sein	*d. to go*
5. heißen	*e. to take*
6. nehmen	*f. to be called*
7. kennen	*g. to live*
8. gehen	*h. to be*
9. reden	*i. to work*

All these verbs are infinitives; you will find the unchanged form of a verb in a dictionary. Take a closer look at the ending of the German infinitives: They almost always end in **–en** like these.

2

Below you find the German personal pronouns.

	Singular	Plural
1st person	**ich** *(I)*	**wir** *(we)*
2nd person	**du** *(you)* familiar form **Sie** *(you)* polite form	**ihr** *(you)* familiar form **Sie** *(you)* polite form
3rd person	**er, sie, es** *(he, she, it)*	**sie** *(they)*

Sie is the polite way to address a stranger or adults who you don't know very well.
Du is used for family, friends, acquaintances and children up to about 16 years.
If you are unsure what to use, use **Sie** and then listen to how the other person addresses you.

Gut zu wissen

Note that **Sie**, when used as the formal form of *you*, always starts with a capital letter.

3 TR. 02

David and his wife introduce themselves to their new neighbour, Thomas Kowalski. Read the dialogue below. You find the dialogue on the CD.

Thomas Kowalski: Ja?
David Simmons: Guten Tag. Wir sind die neuen Nachbarn. Ich heiße David Simmons und das ist meine Frau Melanie.
Thomas Kowalski: Ah, guten Tag. Freut mich! Sie wohnen nebenan, nicht wahr?
David Simmons: Ja, wir wohnen seit letztem Monat hier. Wir kommen aus London und arbeiten jetzt in Düsseldorf.
Thomas Kowalski: Aus London? Das ist ja toll. Moment bitte, ich rufe meine Frau. Sie nimmt Englischunterricht an der Volkshochschule. Susanne, kommst du mal bitte?
Susanne Kowalski: Ja, ich komme.
Thomas Kowalski: Das sind unsere neuen Nachbarn, David und Melanie Simmons.
Susanne Kowalski: Guten Tag. Moment mal, ich kenne Sie doch?
Melanie Simmons: Ja, ich arbeite an der Volkshochschule. Sie sind in meinem Englischkurs.
Susanne Kowalski: Natürlich! Mrs. Simmons! Und das ist ihr Mann. Wie geht es Ihnen Herr Simmons?
David Simmons: Danke, sehr gut. Und Ihnen?
Susanne Kowalski: Ausgezeichnet. Warum kommen Sie nicht auf eine Tasse Kaffee herein. Dann können wir ein bisschen reden.
Melanie und **David Simmons:** Ja, gerne.

4 TR. 03

§ 22 Present tense

You have probably noticed that German verbs can have various endings. The present tense of most verbs in German is formed by adding an ending to the word stem.

For example, **wohnen** (infinitive) – **wohn**- (stem)

ich wohn**e**, du wohn**st**, wir wohn**en**.

If the stem ends in **-t** or **–d** you have to add an **–e** in front of the verb ending in the 2nd and 3rd person singular and the 2nd person plural:

du arbeit-**e-st**, er red-**e-t**, ihr red-**e-t**.

If the stem ends in **–s**, **-ss**, **-ß**, **-z** or **–tz**, leave out the **–s** in the ending for the 2nd person singular:

du heiß-**t**, du sitz-**t**.

NOTE! This applies only for regular verbs!
You can also listen to some examples on the CD.

5

Choose the correct verb form to complete the sentences. All the verbs are regular.

1. Sie *heiße / heißt / heißen* Melanie Simmons.
2. Wir *wohnt / wohne / wohnen* seit einem Monat hier.
3. Er *kommen / kommt / komme* aus London.
4. Ich *arbeitet / arbeiten / arbeite* an der Volkshochschule.
5. Wie *gehe / geht / gehen* es dir Thomas?

Gut zu wissen

There is no way of knowing whether a verb is regular or irregular by looking at its infinitive. When you learn a new verb it helps to write down the infinitive and the third person singular: **geben**, **gibt.**
Or even shorter: **geben**, **i; fahren**, **ä.**

wohnen

ich wohne
du wohnst
er / sie / es wohnt
wir wohnen
ihr wohnt
sie / Sie wohnen

arbeiten

ich arbeite
du arbeitest
er / sie / es arbeitet
wir arbeiten
ihr arbeitet
sie / Sie arbeiten

heißen

ich heiße
du heißt
er / sie / es heißt
wir heißen
ihr heißt
sie / Sie heißen

6 TR.04

Now try to complete the sentences below with the conjugated form of the verbs in brackets. Look at the conjugation box if you aren't sure about the forms. You can also find these sentences on the CD.

1. Ich ________ David Simmons. (heißen)
2. Sie ________ nebenan, nicht wahr? (wohnen)
3. Wir ________ aus London und arbeiten jetzt in Düsseldorf. (kommen)
4. Moment mal, ich ________ Sie doch? (kennen)
5. Ja, ich ________ an der Volkshochschule. (arbeiten)
6. Wie ________ es Ihnen? (gehen)
7. Wir ________ ein bisschen reden. (können)

7 TR.05

Unfortunately a number of verbs are irregular:

Sie **nimmt** Englischunterricht an der Volkshochschule.

These verbs change their stem-vowel in the 2nd and 3rd person singular (Present Tense):

e	▸	ie	as in lesen	▸	du liest, er liest
e	▸	i	as in nehmen	▸	du nimmst, sie nimmt
a	▸	ä	as in fahren	▸	du fährst, er fährt

You can also listen to some examples on the CD.

8

It's your turn now! Try to fill in the gaps with the correct form of **nehmen**, **lesen** and **fahren**.

lesen – *to read*
nehmen – *to take*
fahren – *to go, to drive*

nehmen	lesen	fahren
ich nehme	ich lese	ich fahre
du ________	du ________	du ________
er / sie / es ________	er / sie / es ________	er / sie / es ________
wir nehmen	wir lesen	wir fahren
ihr ________	ihr ________	ihr ________
sie / Sie ________	sie / Sie ________	sie / Sie ________

9

You find another irregular German verb **sein** in the conjugation box on the right. This verb is an exception in German. Look carefully and try to memorize its verb forms. Read the sentences and write the correct form of **sein** in the gaps. Then repeat the complete sentences.

1. Wir ________ die neuen Nachbarn.
2. Das ________ meine Frau Melanie.
3. Ich ________ aus Düsseldorf.
4. Thomas and Melanie ________ aus London.

sein

ich bin
du bist
er / sie / es ist
wir sind
ihr seid
sie / Sie sind

10

Let's take a look at the German personal pronouns. Do you get confused with the words **sie / Sie**? Here are the rules for the usage of **sie** and **Sie**:

§ 19 Personal pronouns

3rd person singular **sie:** pronoun for a single female person or object.

Die Frau ist schön. *The woman is pretty.*	**Sie** ist schön. *She is pretty.*
Die Suppe ist heiß. *The soup is hot.*	**Sie** ist heiß. *It is hot.*

Frau Simmons gibt Englischunterricht.
Sie gibt Englischunterricht.
Mrs Simmons teaches English classes.
She teaches English classes.

3rd person singular **Sie:** pronoun for a single female or male person who you address directly using the polite form of address.

Sie sehen aber sehr gut aus, Frau Meyer!
You look very pretty, Mrs Meyer!
Ja, finden **Sie**?
Really? Do you think so?

3rd person plural **sie:** pronoun for talking about a group of people or objects.

Sie schließen um 20 Uhr. *They close at 8 o'clock.*

3rd person plural **Sie:** pronoun for talking to a group of people using the formal address.

Sind **Sie** die Familie Kowalski? *Are you the Kowalski family?*

11

Read the sentences and write the correct form of **sie / Sie** into the gaps.

1. Ich heiße Thomas Kowalski. Und wie heißen ________?
2. Das sind meine Nachbarn. ________ heißen Simmons.
3. Herr und Frau Simmons, ________ kommen aus London, nicht wahr?
4. Herr Simmons, das ist Susanne, ________ ist meine Frau.
5. Sprechen ________ gut Deutsch, Frau Simmons?

12

▶ § 22 Present tense

Let's go back to the present tense.

The present tense has a broad usage. The sentences on the right explain various uses of the present tense while the sentences on the left are examples. Try to match the explanation with the examples.

1. David ist aus London.
2. Sie lernen Deutsch.
3. Du lernst gerade Deutsch.
4. Susanne trinkt jeden Morgen Kaffee.
5. Thomas arbeitet nicht.
6. Thomas arbeitet morgen nicht.

a. a permanent situation or event
b. a long term situation or event
c. repeated, regular actions in the present
d. actions that happen at the moment
e. future events, activity or plan
f. temporary actions in the present

13

Write the missing conjugated forms of the verbs in present in brackets into the gaps.

1. Guten Tag, Herr Kowalski. Wie ______________ es Ihnen? (gehen)
2. David ______________ Deutsch. (lernen)
3. Thomas ______________ in Düsseldorf. (wohnen)
4. Melanie ______________ aus England. (kommen)
5. Wie ______________ du? (heißen)
6. Wir ______________ neue Nachbarn. (haben)
7. Er ______________ David. (heißen)

14

The words in the following sentences are out of order. Try to put them into the correct order. Then read the sentences aloud. This will help you to improve your pronunciation.

1. morgen / Köln / Thomas / fährt / nach / .

   ____

2. Englisch / Suzanne / morgen / lernt / .

   ____

3. nach / wir / Nächstes Jahr / England / fahren / .

   ____

4. Corinna Beck / Spanien / nach / fährt / nächstes Jahr / .

   ____

5. Urlaub / in zwei Tagen / habt / Ihr / .

   ____

6. du / In zwei Tagen / Urlaub / hast / .

   ____

Gut zu wissen

To express a future plan or activity with the present tense you can use a time expression such as: **morgen** (*tomorrow*), **nächstes Jahr** (*next year*), **in zwei Tagen** (*in two days*).
This time expression can be placed either behind the verb or at the beginning of the sentence.

15 TR. 06

Take a look at these irregular verbs. They all changed their stem vowel **–e-** to **–i-** or **–ie-**. But is it a short or long a long vowel? Below you find some examples:

long **–i-**	short **–i-**
er l**ie**st	es g**i**bt
sie s**ie**ht	du spr**i**chst
	sie n**i**mmt

Now you can also listen to these examples and repeat them aloud for the right pronunciation.

A general rule for long/short vowels is:
long vowels are:

- **i** + **e**(**h**): s**ie**ht, s**ie**
- **e** + **i**: r**ei**sen, h**ei**ßen
- double vowels: St**aa**t (*state*), M**ee**r (*sea*), B**oo**t (*boat*)
- vowel + **h**: f**ah**ren (*to drive*), M**eh**l (*flour*), B**oh**ne (*bean*), **ih**r
- vowel followed by a consonant and another vowel: h**abe**n (*to have*), r**ede**n (*to talk*)

short vowels are:

- vowel followed by two or more consonants: g**ibt**, n**immst**
- vowels at the end of a word: sprech**e**, Bohn**e**

16

Short or long vowel? Read the following verb forms aloud and write them into the right column.

short vowels	long vowels

nehme - gehe - nimmt - liest - gebe - gibt - ist - heißt

personal pronouns

1

Read the following sentences. Which personal pronoun is missing?

1. Someone is talking directly to 3 friends: ________
2. Someone is talking about himself or herself: ________
3. Someone is talking about himself or herself and a friend:

   ____
4. Someone is talking about a male person: ________
5. Someone is talking directly to a friend: ________
6. Someone is talking directly to his/her boss: ________
7. Someone is talking about a female object: ________

2

Write the correct personal pronoun into the gaps. Remember that sentences start with a capital letter.

1. Sind ________ Herr Beck?
2. ________ heiße Melanie Simmons.
3. ________ wohnen in Köln. (Thomas and Susanne)
4. ________ lernst Deutsch.
5. ________ seid David und Melanie.

introducing yourself

die Volkshochschule – *adult education centre*

3

Do you recognise these sentences? Try to match them with their English translations. Read them aloud to practice your pronunciation.

1. Wir sind ihre neuen Nachbarn.
2. Ich heiße David Simmons.
3. Sie wohnen nebenan, nicht wahr?
4. Wir kommen aus London und arbeiten jetzt in Düsseldorf.
5. Sie nimmt Englischunterricht an der Volkshochschule.
6. Moment mal, ich kenne Sie doch?
7. Ja, ich arbeite an der Volkshochschule.
8. Wie geht es Ihnen?

a. She is studying English at the adult education centre.
b. You live next door, don't you?
c. How are you?
d. We are your new neighbours.
e. Wait a minute, don't I know you?
f. Yes, I work at the adult education centre.
g. My name is David Simmons.
h. We come from London and now we work in Düsseldorf.

4

Hidden in the row of letters are sentences which are useful for introducing yourself and others or to ask information about someone. Split the chain of letters so that the sentences are correct. After doing that repeat the sentences aloud.

1. WieheißtDu?
2. IchbinDavid.
3. WirwohneninDüsseldorf.
4. SindSieDeutscher?
5. IchkommeausEngland.
6. SprechenSieDeutsch?
7. WirsprechenDeutschundEnglisch.

1 TR. 08

§ 3 Article - definite

Let's look at the articles. In German, nouns are masculine, feminine or neuter.

Try to match the words to the pictures. If you like you can listen to the words, pronounce them aloud and try to memorize them. Can you guess their English translation? You can listen to these nouns for the proper pronunciation.

der Mann – *man*
die Frau – *woman*
das Kind – *child*
die Tasse – *cup*
das Glas – *glass*
der Tisch – *table*
die Flasche – *bottle*
der Stuhl – *chair*
das Fenster – *window*

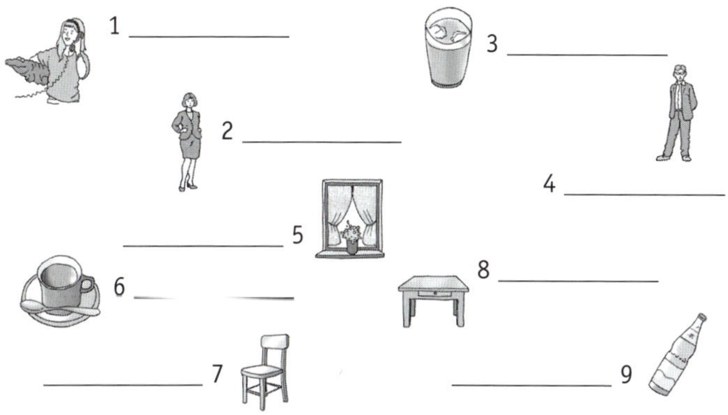

die Tasse - das Glas - der Tisch - die Flasche - der Stuhl - das Fenster - der Mann - die Frau - das Kind

2 TR. 09

§ 4 Article - indefinite

As you know, articles show the gender of a noun and can be either definite (**der**, **die**, **das**) or indefinite (**ein**, **eine**). Look at the following pictures and match them to the correct German sentence. You can also listen to the sentences on the CD.

- a. Das ist ein Mann.
- b. Das ist eine Frau.
- c. Der Mann heißt Thomas.
- d. Die Frau heißt Susanne.

3 TR. 10

Susanne Kowalski invited the Simmons **auf eine Tasse Kaffee.** Look at the picture and read the dialogue. Mark all the articles (definite and indefinite) you can find in the text. You can also listen to the dialogue while reading.

Susanne Kowalski:	So, dann kommen Sie doch bitte herein. Hier entlang, in die Küche.
Thomas Kowalski:	Was dürfen wir Ihnen anbieten? Möchten Sie einen Kaffee oder lieber einen Tee, oder ein Wasser?
David Simmons:	Eine Tasse Kaffee, bitte.
Melanie Simmons:	Und ich nehme ein Wasser.
Susanne Kowalski:	So, hier bitte, das Wasser. Und der Kaffee ... mit Milch und Zucker?
David Simmons:	Nein Danke. Sie haben eine sehr schöne Wohnung.
Thomas Kowalski:	Die Küche ist auch das Wohnzimmer. Wir haben ein Zimmer und das andere Zimmer ist für Lisa.
Melanie Simmons:	Sie haben eine Tochter?
Thomas Kowalski:	Ja, sie hilft gerade der Oma im Garten. Haben Sie Kinder?
Melanie Simmons:	Nein. Wir haben nur eine Katze.
Susanne Kowalski:	Wie gefällt es Ihnen denn in Deutschland?
David Simmons:	In Düsseldorf gefällt es uns gut, aber viele Dinge sind anders. Die Sprache natürlich und das Essen, ...

4

In German, nouns are masculine, feminine or neuter. Articles show the gender of a noun and can be either definite (**der**, **die**, **das**) or indefinite (**ein**, **eine**).

The indefinite article is used when something is new or unknown in the context.

> Das ist **eine** Küche. *This is a kitchen.*

The definite article is used when you talk about a particular thing or person and when it is clear from the context, which thing or person you mean.

> Das ist **die** Küche von Familie Kowalski. *This is the kitchen of the Kowalski family.*

Articles also indicate the number of a noun. The indefinite article has no plural:

> **Die** Wohnungen sind sehr schön. *The flats are very nice.*

5

Now try to fill in the gaps with the correct definite or indefinite article without looking to the dialogue.

1. Möchten Sie ____________ Kaffee oder lieber ____________ Tee, oder ____________ Wasser?
2. ____________ Tasse Kaffee, bitte.
3. So, hier bitte, ____________ Wasser.
4. Sie haben ____________ sehr schöne Wohnung.
5. ____________ Küche ist auch ____________ Wohnzimmer.

6

§ 3 Article - definite

In some cases you don't use an article at all. The following sentences are examples. Match the sentences to the corresponding cases in which you don't use articles at all.

1. Das ist Frau Simmons.
2. Thomas ist Redakteur.
3. Melanie kommt aus England.
4. Thomas ist Deutscher.

a. nationalities
b. countries
c. professions
d. names

Gut zu wissen

Names usually don't use articles. In spoken German however, it is very common, especially in the South of Germany. **(Die) Melanie trinkt keinen Kaffee.**

7

Articles also indicate the case of a noun. There are four different cases in German: nominative, accusative, dative and genitive.

In the accusative case a person/thing does something with another person/thing:

Der Mann trinkt **einen Saft**. *The man drinks some juice.*
Er trinkt **den Saft**. *He drinks the juice.*

Only the masculine article changes.

You need to know the gender of a noun to choose the correct article and to put it into the correct accusative form.

	masculine	feminin	neuter
definite article	**den** Tee	**die** Tochter	**das** Foto
indefinite article	**einen** Tee	**eine** Tochter	**ein** Foto

8 TR. 11

Now try to fill in the gaps with the correct article in the accusative case. You can also listen to these sentences on the CD.

1. Melanie möchte ____________ Tee.
2. David trinkt ____________ Kaffee ohne Zucker.
3. Susanne hat ____________ Tochter.
4. Thomas zeigt ____________ Foto von Lisa.

Verbs that trigger the accusative are for example:

haben, **trinken**, **essen**, **nehmen**, **sehen**, **kaufen** etc.

These are all activities where one person/thing does something directly with another person/thing.

9

Now let's have a look at the dative case.

In the dative case 2 people/things interact:

Susanne gibt **dem** Mann einen Saft.
Susanne passes the man some juice.

Susanne gibt **einem** Mann einen Saft.
Susanne passes a man some juice.

Lisa hilft gerade **der** Oma.
Lisa helps the grandmother.

David hilft **einem** Kind.
David helps a child.

You need to know the gender of a noun to choose the correct article and to put it into the correct dative form.

	masculine	feminin	neuter
definite article	**dem** Mann	**der** Oma	**dem** Kind
indefinite article	**einem** Mann	**einer** Oma	**einem** Kind

Gut zu wissen

Please note the word order:
In a sentence the dative case always comes before the accusative case.

10 TR. 12

Now try to fill in the gaps with the correct article in the dative case. You also find these sentences on the CD.

1. Lisa hilft ____________ Frau.
2. Susanne antwortet ____________ Oma.
3. Oma erklärt ____________ Kind ein Wort.
4. Deutschland gefällt ____________ Simmons.
5. David gibt ____________ Kind einen Saft.
6. Der Wein schmeckt ____________ Mann.

Verbs that trigger the dative are for example:

helfen, bringen, anbieten, geben.

11

Look at the clues and decide which article is needed.
Then write the correct article into the gap.

1. *milk*, female, definite:

   ____________ Milch
2. *bread*, neuter, indefinite:

   ____________ Brot
3. *salad*, masculine, definite:

   ____________ Salat
4. *cheese*, masculine, definite:

   ____________ Käse
5. *wine*, masculine, indefinite:

   ____________ Wein
6. *egg*, neuter, definite:

   ____________ Ei
7. *orange juice*, masculine, indefinite:

   ____________ Orangensaft
8. *pizza*, feminine, definite:

   ____________ Pizza

12 TR. 13

Definite or indefinite article? Write the correct article into the gap to complete the sentences. You can also listen to these sentences and repeat them aloud.

1. Möchtest du ____________ Saft?
2. Ja, gerne. ____________ Orangensaft, bitte.
3. Möchten Sie ____________ Cola?
4. Nein, danke. Ich nehme lieber ____________ Wasser.
5. Trinken Sie ____________ Tee mit Zucker?
6. Ich trinke ____________ Kaffee mit Milch und Zucker.

13

Fill in the correct accusative article. If no article is necessary, leave the gap empty.

1. Haben Sie ____________ Tisch für 3?
2. Haben Sie ____________ Salate?
3. Ich nehme ____________ Salat mit Käse.
4. Ich trinke ____________ Wein.
5. Nehmen Sie ____________ Wein aus Deutschland.
6. Möchten Sie ____________ Flasche Wein?

14

The letters in the words below are all mixed up! Put the letters into the correct order and write them down with the article. You find the clues in the box below.

1. CHEROTT

   ____

2. BHCNARA

   ____

3. CSITH

   ____

4. HLUTS

   ____

5. TERNEFS

   ____

6. SETSA

   ____

7. SLAG

   ____

8. FASHCLE

   ____

neighbour - daughter - table - chair - window - cup - glass - bottle

15

Who is it? Read the following clues about a certain person. Fill in the correct indefinite article or if no article is required leave the gap empty. Write the name of the person into the gap of the last sentence.

1. Sie ist ____________ Frau.
2. Sie hat ____________ Mann.
3. Sie trinkt ____________ Glas Wasser.
4. Sie gibt ____________ Unterricht.
5. Sie ist ____________ Englischlehrerin.
6. Sie kommt aus ____________ London.
7. Sie heißt ____________.

16

Don't worry about the German articles. Here you will get a good overview of the forms and rules.

Complete the rules below by filling the missing forms.

The gender of the noun (masculine, feminine or neuter) is indicated by the article. You have:

1. Definite articles: **der**, **die**, **das**. Plural: ____________
2. Indefinite articles: **ein**, ____________, **ein**.
3. In the accusative case, only the masculine article changes, e.g. ____________ and ____________.
4. No article is used in front of countries, nationalities and names.

1

Article or no article? Read the sentences and underline either the correct article or "-" if no article is necessary.

1. Das ist *die* / *eine* / - Corinna.
2. Thomas ist *die* / - / *ein* Redakteur.
3. Das ist - / *der* / *das* Frau Simmons.
4. Thomas kommt aus *der* / *den* / - Deutschland.
5. Sie haben *das* / *eine* / - Tochter.
6. *Die* / *der* / *das* Tochter heißt Lisa.

2

Let's have a look at some nouns. Read the words below. Do you remember the correct article? Underline the correct article. Repeat them (with the article!) and try to memorize them.

1. *der* / *die* / *das* Flasche
2. *der* / *die* / *das* Wein
3. *der* / *die* / *das* Kind
4. *der* / *die* / *das* Foto
5. *der* / *die* / *das* Käse
6. *der* / *die* / *das* Wohnung
7. *der* / *die* / *das* Milch
8. *der* / *die* / *das* Tee
9. *der* / *die* / *das* Salat
10. *der* / *die* / *das* Glas

articles

3

Choose the correct dative article.

1. Ich gebe *der / den / dem* Mann einen Kaffee.
2. Susanne gibt *der / den / dem* Kind eine Cola.
3. Die Pizza schmeckt *der / den / dem* Frau.
4. Thomas zeigt *der / den / dem* Simmons ein Foto.
5. Wir helfen *einer / einem /* - Mann.
6. Deutschland gefällt *die / den / einen* Simmons.
7. Orangensaft schmeckt *dem / den / das* Kind.

4

What do you order? Complete the sentences using the words given. Start with:

Ich nehme ...

1. die Cola

   ____

2. der Kaffee

   ____

3. der Tee

   ____

4. der Toast

   ____

5. das Bier

   ____

6. der Apfelkuchen

   ____

7. der Wein

   ____

8. das Wasser

   ____

9. der Orangensaft

   ____

1 TR. 14

In this module we take a closer look at the German nouns. Look at the pictures and read the words below. Try to write them into the right gaps. You can also listen to the nouns on the CD.

das Büro - der Stuhl - der Computer - das Telefon - die Firma - die Zeitung - der Kuli - das Papier

1 ____________

2 ____________

3 ____________

4 ____________

5 ____________

6 ____________

7 ____________

8 ____________

2

Read the work places on the left and then the professions on the right. Match the work place to the right profession.

1. die Schule
2. der Supermarkt
3. die Kirche
4. das Geschäft
5. die Apotheke
6. das Restaurant
7. die Bäckerei
8. das Krankenhaus
9. die Metzgerei
10. das Büro

a. die Kassiererin
b. die Sekretärin
c. der Metzger
d. der Kellner
e. der Pfarrer
f. die Lehrerin
g. der Arzt
h. die Verkäuferin
i. der Bäcker
j. die Apothekerin

das Büro - *office*
die Sekretärin - *secretary*
die Bäckerei - *bakery*
der Bäcker - *baker*
die Metzgerei - *butcher's*
der Metzger - *butcher*
das Geschäft - *shop*
die Verkäuferin - *sales assistant*
das Restaurant - *restaurant*
der Kellner - *waiter*
die Schule - *school*
die Lehrerin - *teacher, female*
das Krankenhaus - *hospital*
der Arzt - *doctor*
die Apotheke - *pharmacy*
die Apothekerin - *pharmacist, female*
die Kirche - *church*
der Pfarrer - *priest*
der Supermarkt - *supermarket*
die Kassiererin - *cashier, female*

3

A lot of job titles are masculine and end in -**er**, for example **der** Bäck**er**. To form the female equivalents just add –**in** and change the article: **die** Bäcker**in**. Or the other way round: take off the ending –**in** from a feminine job title to get the masculine version: **die** Verkäufer**in**, **der** Verkäuf**er**.

4

Now try to form the appropriate form of the noun. Don't forget the article!

1. *baker*, female ____________________
2. *butcher*, female ____________________
3. *sales assistant*, male ____________________
4. *waitress*, female ____________________
5. *teacher*, male ____________________
6. *pharmacist*, male ____________________
7. *cashier*, male ____________________

5

§ 12 Nouns - gender

A few rules to recognise the gender of the noun:

Feminine:
Most nouns ending in –**e** are feminine:

die Straß**e** (*street*)
die Fußgängerzon**e** (*pedestrian zone*)
die Kirch**e** (*church*)

BUT there are masculine nouns ending in –**e** as well!

der Junge (*boy*), **der Kollege** (*colleague*)

Pay special attention to them!

Nouns ending in –**ei** are **always** feminine:

die Poliz**ei** (*police*)
die Bäcker**ei** (*bakery*)

Neuter:
All nouns ending in –**um** are neuter:

das Einkaufszentr**um** (*shopping centre*)
das Muse**um** (*museum*)

6 TR. 15

As you already know, each noun has its own gender: *masculine* (**der**), *feminine* (**die**) or *neuter* (**das**). Try to write the following nouns into the right column. You may also listen to these nouns on the CD and practise their pronunciation.

§ 13 Nouns - singular

der	die	das

Gut zu wissen

Days of the week are always masculine: **der Montag, der Sonntag** and colours are always neuter: **das Rot, das Gelb.**

Stadtteil - Rathaus - Museum - Fußgängerzone - Straße - Kino - Parkplatz - Stadtplan - Stadt - Einkaufszentrum - Kirche - Polizei - Park – Geschäft - Bahnhof

7

Most nouns exist in the singular and the plural. Look at the nouns and try to figure out which of them are singular and which are plural. Write them into the corresponding box.

§ 14 Nouns - plural

Singular	Plural

Gut zu wissen

To form the plural for male job titles ending in **-er** just change the article: **der** Bäcker – **die** Bäcker.

der Beruf - die Büros - die Computer - der Kollege - die Firmen - das Büro - die Sekretärinnen - der Computer - die Berufe - die Kollegen - die Sekretärin - die Firma

Now you can complete the following rule:

The plural definite article is always ___________.

8

Gut zu wissen

To form the plural of female job titles ending in **-in** double **-n**, add **-en** and change the article: **die** Bäcker**in** – **die** Bäckerin**nen**.

Below you find several feminine nouns. Try to form their plural forms. Look at the **Gut zu wissen** box on the left for the clue.

1. die Bäckerin ____________________
2. die Sekräterin ____________________
3. die Apothekerin ____________________
4. die Lehrerin ____________________
5. die Ärztin ____________________
6. die Kassiererin ____________________
7. die Kellnerin ____________________

9

Gut zu wissen

There are some words that do not have a plural, for example: **der Urlaub**, **die Polizei**. Likewise there are words without a singular, for example: **die Leute** (*people*), **der Zucker** (*sugar*).

Here you find nouns in plural. Try to put them in singular. Don't forget the correct article.

1. die Bäcker ____________________
2. die Gläser ____________________
3. die Computer ____________________
4. die Kinos ____________________
5. die Männer ____________________
6. die Frauen ____________________
7. die Fotos ____________________
8. die Blumen ____________________
9. die Bahnhöfe ____________________
10. die Parks ____________________

10

Write the plural of the nouns into the gaps.

1. der Supermarkt ______________________
2. die Apotheke ______________________
3. die Straße ______________________
4. die Firma ______________________
5. das Kind ______________________
6. der Stuhl ______________________
7. die Kirche ______________________
8. der Nachbar ______________________
9. der Stadtplan ______________________
10. der Lehrer ______________________

Gut zu wissen

If there's a vowel **a**, **o**, **u** in the noun, it is mostly changed to **ä**, **ö**, **ü**.

11

Surely you remember that the article of a noun can change according to the case:

Das ist **der** Mann. (nominative)
Ich sehe **den** Mann. (accusative)

Nouns can also change according to the case: in the dative plural all nouns add an –**n**.
Look at the table below:

	masculine	feminine	neuter
nominative	die Männer	die Frauen	die Kinder
accusative	die Männer	die Frauen	die Kinder
dative	den Männer**n**	den Frauen	den Kinder**n**

Gut zu wissen

Most feminine nouns in the plural already end in –**n** so they don't add an extra –**n** in the dative case. Plural nouns that end in –**s** (**Büros**, **Restaurants**) don't add an –**n** either.

12 TR. 16

Now try to fill in the following gaps. All nouns in the brackets should be either in the dative or the accusative case. You can also find these sentences on the CD.

1. Der Mann sieht ________________. (Kinder)
2. Der Lehrer hilft ________________. (Kinder)
3. Der Kellner begrüßt ________________. (Frauen)
4. Der Kellner bringt ________________ die Speisekarte. (Frauen)
5. ________________ sind krank. (Männer)
6. Der Arzt hilft ________________. (Männer)

13

Translate the noun in brackets and write its dative form into the gap.

1. Die Mutter gibt dem ________________ das Essen. (*boy*)
2. Der Vater spricht mit den ________________. (*children*)
3. Die Mutter bringt den ________________ das Essen. (*daughters*)
4. Susanne bringt dem ________________ Blumen. (*neighbour*)
5. Thomas und David arbeiten mit den ________________. (*computers*)
6. Der Lehrer spricht mit den ________________. (*children*)
7. Der Arzt hilft den ________________. (*men*)
8. Carola schreibt den ________________. (*women*)
9. David gibt dem ________________ einen Kaffee. (*colleague*)

14

§ 9 Masculine nouns in **-e**

Masculine singular nouns that end in –**e** follow the so called **n-declination pattern**.
In all cases and numbers the nouns of the n-declination take an –**n** ending.
Only the nominative singular does not take an –**n**.

	masculine	plural
nominative	der Kollege	die Kollegen
accusative	den Kollege**n**	die Kollegen
dative	dem Kollege**n**	den Kollegen

15 TR. 17

Try to fill in the gaps with the correct form of the noun **Kollege** together with the proper article. You can also listen to these sentences on the CD.

1. Das sind __________________ im Büro. (*plural*)
2. Ich habe auch __________________ aus Frankreich. (*singular*)
3. Das ist __________________ aus Frankreich, Henry Dufour. (*singular*)
4. Ich spreche oft mit __________________ Dufour. (*singular*)
5. Ich helfe __________________ viel. (*plural*)
6. Ich sehe __________________ im Büro. (*plural*)

Other words that follow this pattern are all masculine nouns ending in –**e:**
der Jung**e** (*boy*), der Buchstab**e** (*letter*), der Nam**e** (*name*),
and some others like:
der Nachbar (*neighbour*), **der Herr** (*gentleman or Mr*), **der Bauer** (*farmer*), **der Student** (*student*).

16 TR. 18

The German language has some pretty long words most of which are compound words, nouns that are composed of two or more other nouns. These compound nouns take the article of the last noun. For example:

der Kaffee + **die** Tasse = **die** Kaffetasse

Look at the pictures. Then match the nouns on the left with the ones on the right and write them into the gap under the appropriate picture. Don't forget the article. You can also listen to these words on the CD.

1 ______________

2 ______________

3 ______________

4 ______________

5 ______________

Büro	Teil
Computer	Name
Stadt	Tür
Haus	Stuhl
Straßen	Geschäft
Blumen	Tisch

6 ______________

17

Look at the pictures and write the professions with their article into the gap. Example: **der Chef** or **die Chefs** if there is more than one.

1 ______________

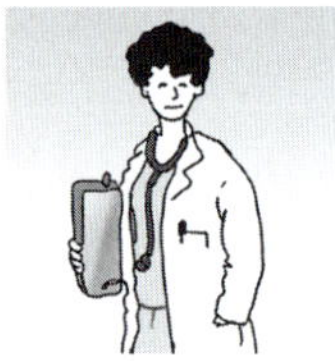

2 ______________

3 ______________

4 ______________

5 ______________

gender of nouns

1

Do you remember the features that help you to recognise the gender of a noun? Mark the correct answer.

1. Job titles in –**er** are
   - a. masculine.
   - b. feminine.
   - c. neuter.

2. The days of the week are
   - a. masculine.
   - b. feminine.
   - c. neuter.

3. Colours are
   - a. masculine.
   - b. feminine.
   - c. neuter.

4. Nouns in –**in** are
   - a. masculine.
   - b. feminine.
   - c. neuter.

2

Match the words to the correct translations.

1. die Kinos	*a. street names*
2. die Kirchen	*b. houses*
3. die Städte	*c. shops*
4. die Häuser	*d. churches*
5. die Straßennamen	*e. cinemas*
6. die Geschäfte	*f. cities*

compound words

3

Find the compound words in the letter chain and underline them.

1. *flower shop*

   IKGRTZBLUMENGESCHÄFTIE

2. *office chair*

   BÜROSTUHLMUNKCON

3. *table for the computer*

   IMUSCOMPUTERTISCHTR

4. *city map*

   SCDFESTADTPLANHUFGTD

5. *menu*

   LSPEISEKARTEEURSRE

6. *coffee cup*

   JIEÖSKAFFEETASSEHNBERT

7. *street name*

   ZIHGENSTRAßENNAME

4

Choose the correct form of the noun to complete the sentences and underline them in each sentence.

1. Das ist *ein Junge / einen Jungen / ein Jungen*.
2. Der Junge hat *eine Name / einen Namen / ein Name*.
3. Ich habe *ein Beruf / einen Berufe / einen Beruf*.
4. Der Kellner bringt *dem Männer / den Männer / den Männern* ein Wasser.
5. Ich habe 2 *Töchter / Töchtern / Tochter*.

1 TR. 19

In this module we take a closer look at the separable verbs. Read the infinitives on the left hand side and the sentences on the right hand side. Each of the sentences contains the conjugated form of an infinitive verb on the left. Pay attention, some of them consist of two parts. Match the verbs with the corresponding sentence. Pay special attention to the verb and the word at the end of each sentence. You can also listen to the verbs on the CD.

§ 24 Separable verbs

1. einkaufen
2. ausgeben
3. mitkommen
4. einladen
5. anrufen
6. absagen
7. mitbringen
8. aufessen
9. vorschlagen
10. aufräumen

a. Bringst du Schokolade mit?
b. David räumt die Küche auf.
c. Er isst alles auf.
d. Melanie schlägt etwas anderes vor.
e. Sie gibt viel Geld aus.
f. Die Kowalskis sagen ab.
g. Melanie kauft im Supermarkt ein.
h. David ruft Thomas an.
j. David kommt nicht mit.
i. Sie laden die Kowalskis zum Essen ein.

einkaufen – *to shop*
ausgeben – *to spend money*
mitkommen – *to come along*
einladen – *to invite*
anrufen – *to call*
absagen – *to decline (an invitation)*
mitbringen – *to bring along*
aufessen – *to eat up*
vorschlagen – *to suggest*
aufräumen – *to tidy up*

2

These verbs are separable verbs, i.e.: they have a separable prefix that goes to the end of the sentence when the verb is conjugated.

3 TR. 20

▶ § 24 Separable verbs

Melanie is going shopping. Read the dialogue below and underline the separable verbs you find in the dialogue. You can also listen to this dialogue on the CD.

Gut zu wissen

In some cases (subordinate clause, Perfect Tense, with modal verbs) the prefix and the verb do not separate. Check the grammar section for more details.

David: Kaufst du viel ein?
Melanie: Na ja, wir brauchen Nudeln, Fisch, Gemüse, Wein, Salat und noch so ein paar andere Sachen. Ich will Thomas und Susanne morgen zum Essen einladen.
David: Das ist eine gute Idee. Bringst du auch Schokolade mit?
Melanie: Du willst nicht mitkommen?
David: Nein, ich bleibe lieber hier und ruhe etwas aus.
Melanie: Aha, du ruhst etwas aus und ich muss einkaufen.
David: Nicht?
Melanie: Ich schlage etwas anderes vor: Du räumst die Küche auf und wäschst das Geschirr ab. Dann bringe ich auch Schokolade mit.
David: Jawohl, Chef. Noch etwas?
Melanie: Rufe auch bitte die Kowalskis an und lade sie ein.
David: Natürlich, ich rufe Thomas gleich an. Was kochst du?
Melanie: Fisch mit Gemüse und Nudeln. Hoffentlich essen sie Fisch …
David: Ich frage nach. Hoffentlich sagen sie ab.
Melanie: Warum denn?
David: Dann esse ich alles alleine auf! Na ja, vielleicht gebe ich Lisa etwas ab.
Melanie: Ich gehe dann los.
David: Gib nicht zu viel Geld aus und vergiss meine Schokolade nicht.
Melanie: Ja, Chef.

4 TR. 21

Separable verbs are verbs that consist of 2 parts: a prefix and the verb. The prefix changes the meaning of the verb:

aufmachen	**zu**machen

In the infinitive form, the prefix and verb are one word, but in statements and questions the separable prefix moves to the very end of the sentence.

aufmachen:	Ich **mache** die Tür **auf**. *I open the door.*
zumachen:	**Mach** bitte die Tür **zu**. *Please close the door.*

In spoken German, the separable prefix is always the syllable that is stressed in a word. You also find these examples on the CD.

5 TR. 22

In the box below you find a few of the most common prefixes. Complete the sentences by putting the correct one at the end of the sentence. Look at the box on the right for the clues. You also find these sentences on the CD.

nach- ab- auf- weg- zu- an-

1. David fängt morgen mit einer Diät ____________.
2. Wir lehnen strenge Diäten ____________.
3. Sylvia hört mit dem Rauchen ____________.
4. Wir denken über eine gesunde Ernährung ____________.
5. Ich lasse Fleisch einfach ____________.
6. Melanie isst viel aber sie nimmt nie ____________.

zunehmen – *to gain weight*
weglassen – *to leave out*
nachdenken – *to think*
aufhören – *to quit*
ablehnen – *to disapprove*
anfangen – *to start*

6

The words in the following sentences are mixed up. Put the words into the correct order. Remember that the prefixes of separable verbs go to the very end of the sentence.

1. Supermarkt / Susanne / ein / kauft / im / .

   ____

2. viel Geld / aus / Sie / gibt / .

   ____

3. kommt / David / mit / nicht / .

   ____

4. Schokolade / Bringst / mit / du / ?

   ____

5. vor / Melanie / etwas anderes / schlägt / .

   ____

6. die Küche / David / auf / räumt / .

   ____

7 TR. 23

Some verbs have a prefix that is not separable. Prefixes **be**-, **ver**-, **ge**-, **er**-, **em**- are never separable.

Unlike separable prefixes (**ab**-, **an**-, **ein**-, **aus**- etc.), inseparable prefixes are **not** stressed in spoken German.

Now try to complete the table by putting the verbs into the right column. If you want you can also listen to these verbs paying special attention if the prefixes are stressed or not stressed.

inseparable verbs	separable verbs

mitbringen - ausruhen - bezahlen - genießen - empfehlen - umrühren - erklären - einkaufen - vergessen

8 TR. 24

Mr Koch explains one of his favourite German dishes: **Bratwürstchen mit Kartoffelsalat.** Look at the pictures and try to match them with Mr Koch's explanations. Write the letter of the correct one into the gap. You can also find these explanations on the CD.

Gut zu wissen

Mr Koch uses the formal imperative.

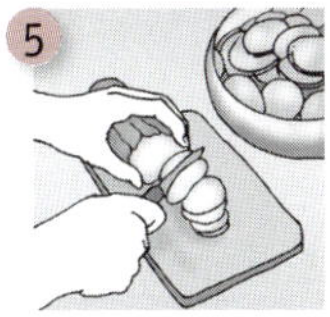

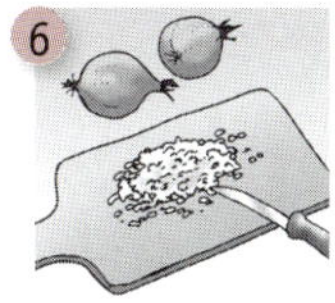

- ■ a. Kochen Sie die Kartoffeln.
- ■ b. Würzen Sie mit Salz.
- ■ c. Braten Sie die Würstchen.
- ■ d. Schneiden Sie die Kartoffeln.
- ■ e. Kaufen Sie Bratwürstchen.
- ■ f. Trinken Sie kaltes Bier zum Essen.
- ■ g. Guten Appetit!
- ■ h. Geben Sie Zwiebeln dazu.
- ■ i. Geben Sie Fett in eine Pfanne.
- ■ j. Rühren Sie gut um.

9 TR. 25

The imperative is used to give instructions or orders, to advice or to suggest. There are several imperative forms and all are derived from the present tense.

§ 7 Imperative

du (informal): take the corresponding verb in the present tense (**du gehst**), omit the personal pronoun **du** and the ending –**st**. **Geh!** *Go!*

Sie (formal): **Sie gehen**, just invert the word order. **Gehen Sie!** *Go!*

If you are part of a group use the **wir**-imperative: take **wir gehen** and just invert the order. **Gehen wir!** *Let's go!*

If you are addressing a group of people use the imperative for **ihr**: **ihr geht**, omit the personal pronoun. **Geht!** *Go!*

If the verb is irregular in the present tense, the **du**-imperative is also irregular: essen ▸ **Iss!**

Separable verbs are also separable in the imperative: umrühren ▸ **Rühren** Sie **um!**

The examples above are also included on the CD.

10

Read some excellent advice from our health specialist Dr. Ernesta Fit-Fiedler. She uses the informal imperative. Then try to put the following sentences into the formal imperative.

Example: **Geh**! - **Gehen Sie**.

1. Trink viel Wasser.

   ____

2. Iss mehr Fisch.

   ____

3. Hör mit dem Rauchen auf.

   ____

4. Kauf viel Gemüse.

   ____

5. Vergiss Diäten.

   ____

11

Be bossy and give orders. Change the given sentences into the imperative.

Example: **Du isst Nudeln**. – **Iss Nudeln!**

1. Du isst Fisch.

   ____

2. Du trinkst Milch.

   ____

3. Du kochst Kaffee.

   ____

4. Du gehst ins Kino.

   ____

5. Du isst Gemüse.

   ____

6. Du räumst die Küche auf.

   ____

12

Below you find a list of things you want your friends to do. Write complete sentences using the imperative. Remember: you have to omit the personal pronoun!

Gut zu wissen
Separable verbs are also separable in the imperative.

1. die Tür zumachen ______________________________
2. Schokolade mitbringen ______________________________
3. das Gemüse nicht vergessen ______________________________
4. Bratwürstchen kaufen ______________________________
5. die Küche aufräumen ______________________________
6. das Geschirr abwaschen ______________________________

13

Bitte, **doch** and **mal** make an imperative sound less bossy.
Doch and **mal** do not have a meaning of their own in this case.

Doch is especially used in suggestions or advice.

If you use two or all three softeners the order is always **doch** – **bitte** - **mal** or **doch** - **mal**/**bitte**.

Bitte is positioned after the verb or at the beginning of the sentence.

14 TR. 26

Now try to make the sentences below more polite using **doch**, **mal** or **bitte**. There is more than one solution possible. You can also listen to some sample sentences on the CD.

1. Trink nicht so viel. ______________________________
2. Wasch das Geschirr ab. ______________________________
3. Ruf Melanie an. ______________________________
4. Komm mit. ______________________________
5. Denk nach. ______________________________
6. Ruh dich mehr aus. ______________________________

15

Read the translation of the German verb which is hidden in the row of letters. Find the verb and write it into the gap.

1. *to forget*

   mkldkfeovergessendkgfoeik ________________

2. *to pay*

   ojtggekwwbezahlenokdkrfkk ________________

3. *to invite*

   iroegjewjeinladenkolwor ________________

4. *to call*

   ijznfgoanrufenpopkgohäöüws ________________

5. *to shop*

   hinenpaeinkaufenlpoenjik ________________

6. *to rest*

   klskdoausruhenkiskdiogjrifseo ________________

7. *to close*

   sjkkfoigjzumachenjkhjgfkef ________________

8. *to quit*

   lasofjkjbiaufhörenmkoeowi ________________

Two of the verbs are inseparable. Do you know which ones? Write them into the gaps below.

a. ____________ b. ____________

16

Let's once again look at the prefixes. You know they can be separable or inseparable. Try to write the prefixes you find in the box into the right column.

separable prefixes	**inseparable prefixes**

zu- nach- em- ver- an- vor- be- ein- er- mit- ge- aus-

1

Complete the rules below by marking the correct answer.

1. Separable prefixes are
   - a. always stressed.
   - b. never stressed.
   - c. sometimes stressed.

2. Inseparable prefixes are
   - a. always stressed.
   - b. never stressed.
   - c. sometimes stressed.

3. In a sentence the prefix is
   - a. behind the verb.
   - b. at the end of the sentence.
   - c. in front of the verb.

4. The correct **ihr**-imperative is
   - a. **kommt.**
   - b. **ihr kommt.**
   - c. **kommt ihr.**

5. The **du**-imperative
   - a. uses the pronoun **du.**
   - b. drops **du** and ending **–st.**
   - c. uses the ending **–st.**

6. For the **Sie**-imperative
   - a. invert pronoun and verb.
   - b. drop the ending **–en.**
   - c. drop the pronoun **Sie.**

2

The letters of the following prefix verbs (infinitives) are mixed up. Put the letters into correct order. The first letter is already given. You find the English translations in the vocabulary box on the right.

1. AERNNUF ____________________
2. ANGEEBB ____________________
3. WSSANLEGE ____________________
4. UÜHRERNM ____________________
5. MKMMOITEN ____________________
6. AENÄFRMUU ____________________

1. to call
2. to hand sth to sb
3. to leave sth out
4. to stir
5. to come along
6. to tidy up

imperative - separable verbs

3

Read the German sentences on the left and match them with the corresponding translation on the right.

1. Erklären Sie das bitte.
2. Esst auf!
3. Laden wir die Kowalskis ein!
4. Kommen Sie mit!
5. Essen Sie mehr Nudeln!
6. Ruf Thomas an!
7. Lade Lisa ein!
8. Trinkt viel Wasser!
9. Rühren Sie gut um!
10. Hören Sie mit dem Rauchen auf!
11. Lass das Fleisch weg!
12. Gib Lisa etwas ab!
13. Schlag etwas anderes vor!
14. Vergiss Diäten!

a. Leave out the meat!
b. Suggest something else!
c. Hand something to Lisa.
d. Invite Lisa!
e. Stir well!
f. Let's invite the Kowalskis!
g. Quit smoking!
h. Forget diets!
i. Drink lots of water!
j. Eat more pasta!
k. Come along!
l. Call Thomas!
m. Please explain that.
n. Eat up!

4

Complete the sentences by writing the missing (conjugated) verb into the gaps.

kaufen - kommen - geben - rühren - schlagen - bringen

1. Melanie ____________________ Gemüse ein.
2. ____________________ du Schokolade mit?
3. David ____________________ Lisa etwas ab.
4. ____________________ doch etwas anderes vor!
5. Herr Koch ____________________ den Salat um.
6. David ____________________ nicht mit.

1 TR. 27

Melanie tells Susanne about her summer trip to Italy. What have she and David done there? Look at the pictures and try to match them with the corresponding sentence from the box below. You can also listen to the sentences on the CD.

1
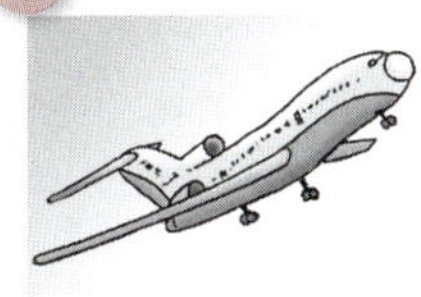
___

2

___

3

___

4

___

5

___

6
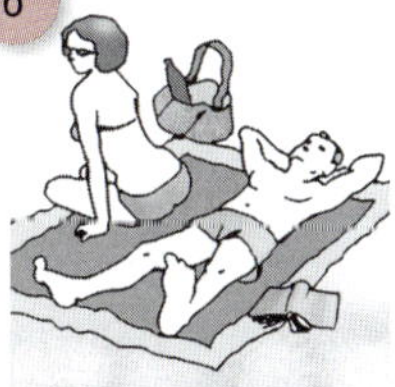
___

a. Wir haben Ausflüge gemacht.
b. Wir haben Pizza gegessen.
c. Wir sind geflogen.
d. Wir sind im Meer geschwommen.
e. Wir haben nette Leute getroffen.
f. Wir haben am Strand gelegen.

2

In this module we deal with the Perfect Tense. The Perfect Tense is a compound tense: conjugated form of **haben** (*to have*) or **sein** (*to be*) + **past participle**. Here's a little reminder of the forms of **haben** and **sein**:

sein (*to be*)	**haben** (*to have*)
ich bin	ich habe
du bist	du hast
er / sie / es ist	er / sie / es hat
wir sind	wir haben
ihr seid	ihr habt
sie / Sie sind	sie / Sie haben

3 TR. 28

The Kowalski's are about to leave for a well deserved vacation. Read the dialogue about the preparations they have made before leaving. You can also listen to this dialogue on the CD.

Susanne: So, ... ist alles fertig?
Thomas: Ja, wir sind startklar.
Susanne: Moment mal ... Haben wir auch die Pässe?
Thomas: Ja, die Pässe und die Flugtickets habe ich in meine Tasche gesteckt.
Susanne: Hast du die Blumen gegossen?
Thomas: Ich habe die Blumen gegossen und ich habe den Simmons den Schlüssel gegeben. Sie gießen die Blumen, wenn wir in Mexiko sind.
Susanne: Die Kaffeemaschine! Ach nein, die habe ich ja schon ausgemacht. Aber ich habe bestimmt noch etwas vergessen ...
Thomas: Nein, du hast bestimmt nichts vergessen. Wir haben die Koffer gepackt. Wir haben den Reiseführer eingepackt. Du hast literweise Sonnencreme gekauft. Ich habe ein Taxi gerufen.
Susanne: Aber irgendwie habe ich das Gefühl ...
Thomas: Ach Susanne! Komm, wir müssen los. Wir verpassen sonst das Flugzeug.
Susanne: Na ja ... gut.
Lisa: Mama, Papa?
Susanne: Oh, nein! Wir haben Lisa vergessen!

4

The perfect tense **das Perfekt** is the most frequently used past tense in German. It consists of two parts: a form of **haben** (*to have*) or **sein** (*to be*) in the present tense and the **past participle** (**gekauft**, **gespielt**, ...).

Most verbs form the **Perfekt** with the auxiliary **haben**, while verbs that indicate motion like **laufen** (*to walk*), **wegfahren** (*to go/to drive away*), **schwimmen** (*to swim*), however, form the **Perfekt** with **sein**.

5

buchen – gebucht
schwimmen – geschwommen
liegen – gelegen
wegfahren - weggefahren

Complete the sentences by writing the forms of **haben** or **sein** into the gaps.

1. Wir ____________ eine Reise nach Mexiko gebucht.
2. Susanne ____________ am Strand gelegen.
3. Lisa ____________ im Meer geschwommen.
4. ____________ Sie auch weggefahren?

6

Thomas is telling Susanne what he is doing at the moment. He is using the present tense. Read the sentences on the left and then look for the corresponding sentence in the perfect tense and match the two together.

1. Ich gieße die Blumen.
2. Ich gebe den Simmons den Schlüssel.
3. Ich packe die Koffer.
4. Ich packe den Reiseführer ein.
5. Ich rufe ein Taxi.

a. Ich habe ein Taxi gerufen.
b. Ich habe die Blumen gegossen.
c. Ich habe den Reiseführer eingepackt.
d. Ich habe den Simmons den Schlüssel gegeben.
e. Ich habe die Koffer gepackt.

7 TR. 29

Read the German sentences on the left and try to match them with the correct translation on the right. You can also find these sentences on the CD.

§ 18 Perfect tense

1. Die Kowalskis haben eine Reise gebucht.
2. Thomas hat die Flugtickets gekauft.
3. Susanne hat die Koffer gepackt.
4. Ich habe den Simmons den Schlüssel gegeben.
5. Du hast die Pässe in die Tasche gesteckt.
6. Wir haben ein Taxi gerufen.
7. Haben wir etwas vergessen?

a. You have put the passports into the bag.
b. We have called a taxi.
c. Have we forgotten something?
d. The Kowalskis have booked a trip.
e. Thomas has bought the tickets.
f. I have given the key to the Simmons.
g. Susanne has packed the suitcases.

past participle

8

▸ § 18 Perfect tense

Regular verbs form the participle as follows:

ge + stem of the verb + **t**

reisen:	**ge**-reis-**t**
	Wir sind nach Italien gereist.
	We have travelled to Italy.
likewise:	spielen – **ge**spiel**t**
	kaufen – **ge**kauf**t**
	hören – **ge**hör**t**
	machen – **ge**mach**t**
	packen – **ge**pack**t**

arbeiten:	**ge**arbeite**t**
ends in -**et** because the stem of the verb ends in -**t**	
	Wir haben nicht gearbeit**et**.
	We haven't worked.
likewise:	reden – **ge**rede**t**
	heiraten – **ge**heirate**t**

einkaufen:	ein**ge**kauf**t**
Regular separable verbs insert the –**ge** between the prefix and the stem.	
	Wir haben Souvenirs ein**ge**kauft.
	We have bought souvenirs.
likewise:	einpacken – ein**ge**packt
	ausmachen –aus**ge**macht
	einstecken – ein**ge**steckt

9 TR. 30

Read the sentences below paying special attention to the participle at the end of the sentence. Look at the pictures and decide which sentence belongs to which picture. You may also listen to these sentences.

1

___

2

___

3

___

a. Wir haben nicht gearbeitet.
b. Wir sind nach Italien gereist.
c. Wir haben Souvenirs eingekauft.

10

Now you know the rules, try to form the past participle of the regular verbs in brackets.

1. Ich habe ein Flugticket ____________________. (kaufen)
2. Sie sind nach Mexiko ____________________. (reisen)
3. David hat Volleyball ____________________. (spielen)
4. Ich habe 4 Koffer ____________________. (packen)
5. Sie haben ____________________. (heiraten)

11

Thomas has a surprise for Susanne and Lisa: he booked a trip to Mexico. Match the sentences with the correct infinitive and take a good look at the participle at the end of the sentence. All these verbs are irregular. Look at the **Gut zu wissen** box on the right to see how they form the past participle.

Gut zu wissen

Past participle of irregular verbs: **ge-** + often changed stem + **en**.

1. Heute bin ich in ein Reisebüro gegangen.
2. Ich habe Kataloge angesehen.
3. Ich habe mit dem Mitarbeiter gesprochen.
4. Er hat mir eine Reise nach Mexiko empfohlen.
5. Das Hotel und der Preis haben mir gut gefallen.
6. Wir sind noch nie nach Mexiko geflogen.
7. Und ich habe immer gerne Tequila getrunken.
8. Ich habe mich schnell entschlossen und gebucht.
9. Die Tickets habe ich gleich mitgenommen.

a. fliegen
b. trinken
c. mitnehmen
d. gefallen
e. ansehen
f. empfehlen
g. entschließen
h. sprechen
i. gehen

1. Today I went to the travel agency.
2. I have looked at the catalogues.
3. I have talked to the employee.
4. He has recommended a trip to Mexico.
5. I have really liked the hotel and the price.
6. We have never flown to Mexico.
7. And I have always liked to drink Tequila.
8. I have decided quickly and booked.
9. I have taken the tickets right away.

12 TR. 31

> **Gut zu wissen**
> Verbs with inseparable prefixes never take **ge**-. Separable verbs insert the **-ge-** between the prefix and the stem.

Some participles are so called 'mixed forms' because they change their stem vowel like participles of irregular verbs but take the ending -(**e**)**t** like participles of regular verbs.

The participles of **mitbringen** (*to bring*), **verbringen** (*to spend time*), **kennen** (*to know*) and **denken** (*to think*) are such mixed forms. You also find these verbs together with their past participle forms on the CD.

13

Now try to complete the sentences by writing the correct participle of the verbs given in brackets into the gap. You find the forms in the box below.

1. Wir haben 2 Wochen in Italien ________________. (verbringen)
2. Melanie hat Italien noch nicht ________________. (kennen)
3. Wir haben viel an euch ________________. (denken)
4. Wir haben euch ein Souvenir ________________. (mitbringen)

mitgebracht - gekannt - verbracht - gedacht

14

> **Gut zu wissen**
> The past participle is always at the very end of the sentence!

The words in the following sentences are mixed up. Put them into the correct order. For a little help, check the **Gut zu wissen** box on the left.

1. Ich / ein Flugticket / gekauft / habe / .

   ____

2. gereist / Mexiko / Sie / nach / sind / .

   ____

3. hat / David / gespielt / Volleyball / .

   ____

4. Italien / uns / gefallen / hat / .

   ____

5. den Simmons / habe/ Ich / gegeben / den Schlüssel / .

   ____

6. Kataloge / angesehen / habe / Ich / .

   ____

15

Read the infinitives in brackets and write the correct past participle into the gap. The picture on the right will help you.

1. Ich habe viel ____________________. (arbeiten)
2. Er hat eine Reise ____________________. (buchen)
3. Wir haben viele Souvenirs ____________________. (kaufen)
4. Sie haben ____________________. (heiraten)
5. Sie hat Ausflüge ____________________. (machen)
6. Du hast den Reiseführer ____________________. (einpacken)
7. Sie hat die Kaffeemaschine ____________________. (ausmachen)
8. Ihr habt viel ____________________. (einkaufen)

16

And what about the participle of irregular verbs? Write the correct past participle of the verbs in brackets into the gaps. Again, the picture on the right will help you.

1. Ich bin ____________________. (gehen)
2. Er hat ____________________. (sprechen)
3. Sie hat viel ____________________. (essen)
4. Wir haben Wein ____________________. (trinken)
5. Ihr seid nach Italien ____________________. (fliegen)
6. Sie haben einen Film ____________________. (ansehen)
7. Ihr habt Lisa ____________________. (mitnehmen)
8. Die Kowalskis sind ____________________. (wegfahren)

17

Gut zu wissen

Verbs that indicate motion form the perfect with the auxiliary **sein**.

Most verbs form the perfect with the auxiliary **haben** and only some with **sein**. Read the sentences and write the correct form of **haben** or **sein** into the gap.

1. Das Hotel __________________ uns gefallen.
2. __________________ ihr nach Italien geflogen?
3. Wir __________________ mit dem Auto gefahren.
4. Susanne __________________ einen Ausflug gemacht.
5. Du __________________ nicht weggefahren.
6. Viele Touristen __________________ nach Mexiko geflogen.
7. Ich __________________ eine Reise nach Spanien gebucht.

18

You want to know all about your friend's vacation. Write the missing participles from the box below into the gaps.

1. Hat dir das Hotel __________________?
2. Hast du Postkarten __________________?
3. Hast du Sonnencreme __________________?
4. Hast du Ausflüge __________________?
5. Bist du im Meer __________________?
6. Hast du in der Disco __________________?
7. Hast du am Strand __________________?

gemacht - gefallen - geschrieben - getanzt - gelegen - geschwommen - gekauft

1

Complete the rules below by marking the correct answer in the box.

1. The past participle of **sehen** is
   - a. **geseht.**
   - b. **gesehen.**
   - c. **seht.**

2. Verbs that indicate motion form
   - a. the past participle with **sein.**
   - b. the past participle with **haben.**
   - c. the past participle with **sein** and **haben.**

3. Verbs with a separable prefix add
   - a. **ge**- before the prefix.
   - b. don't take **ge**-.
   - c. **ge**- between prefix and stem.

4. The past participle of irregular verbs
   - a. end in –**t.**
   - b. end in –**en.**
   - c. never add **ge**-.

2

Look at the following verbs. Do you know how to form their past participle? Which of them take –**ge**- and which don't? Write them into the correct table.

participle with ge-	participle without ge-

buchen - empfehlen - ausmachen - fotografieren - vergessen - entschließen - wegfahren - spielen - gefallen - arbeiten - geben - verreisen

Gut zu wissen

Verbs that end in –**ieren** and verbs with inseparable prefixes never take **ge**- to form the perfect tense.

perfect tense - auxiliary verbs

3 TR. 32

Look at the pictures below. What have the people in the pictures done? Mark the correct answer. You can also find the sentences on the CD.

1

- a. Wir haben Ausflüge gemacht.
- b. Ich habe in der Disco getanzt.
- c. Wir sind im Meer geschwommen.

2

- a. Wir haben nette Leute getroffen.
- b. Ich habe in der Disco getanzt.
- c. Er hat Souvenirs gekauft.

3

- a. Wir haben nette Leute getroffen.
- b. Wir sind im Meer geschwommen.
- c. Wir haben Pizza gegessen.

4

- a. Wir sind geflogen.
- b. Wir sind im Meer geschwommen.
- c. Ich habe Postkarten geschrieben.

4

Write the correct form of **haben** or **sein** into the gaps.

1. Ihr ____________ nach Italien gefahren.
2. Die Kowalskis ____________ Ausflüge gemacht.
3. Die Simmons ____________ nach Mexiko geflogen.
4. Sylvia ____________ nicht weggefahren.
5. Du ____________ viel gegessen.
6. Ich ____________ im Meer geschwommen.
7. Ich ____________ 4 Koffer gepackt.
8. Ihr ____________ ein Ticket gekauft.

1 TR. 33

Lisa is only eight years old. There are a lot of things she can do, she likes or wants to do, many things she is not allowed to do and even a few things she has to do or should do. Look at the pictures and try to match them with the corresponding sentence from the box below. You can also listen to the sentences on the CD.

§ 10 Modal verbs

- a. Lisa mag Nikolas.
- b. Lisa will Nikolas heiraten.
- c. Lisa soll viel Gemüse essen.
- d. Lisa darf nicht arbeiten.
- e. Lisa kann Spaghetti kochen.
- f. Lisa muss ihr Zimmer aufräumen.

2

In this module we deal with the modal verbs. The forms you see in the sentences above (**mag**, **kann**, **muss**, **soll**, **darf** und **will**) are conjugated forms (3rd person singular) of the infinitives **mögen**, **können**, **müssen**, **sollen**, **dürfen** and **wollen**. You find the translations in the word box.

mögen – *to like*
können – *can, could*
dürfen – *may, to be allowed*
müssen – *must, to have to*
sollen – *shall, should*
wollen – *to want*

3 TR. 34

Now you know the meaning of the verbs, try to match the German sentences on the left with the translation on the right.
You can also find these sentences on the CD.

1. Lisa kann Rad fahren.
2. Lisa darf nicht arbeiten.
3. Lisa muss zur Schule gehen.
4. Lisa mag Nikolas.
5. Lisa soll viel Gemüse essen.
6. Lisa darf bis 21 Uhr lesen.
7. Lisa muss ihr Zimmer aufräumen.
8. Lisa kann Spaghetti kochen.
9. Lisa will Nikolas heiraten.

a. Lisa is not allowed to work.
b. Lisa can cook spaghetti.
c. Lisa likes Nikolas.
d. Lisa shall/should eat a lot of vegetables.
e. Lisa has to tidy up her room.
f. Lisa is allowed to read until 9 pm.
g. Lisa wants to marry Nikolas.
h. Lisa can ride a bike.
i. Lisa has to go to school.

4

können

ich kann
du kannst
er / sie / es kann
wir können
ihr könnt
sie / Sie können

Let's start with the first modal verb **können**.
What can the people in the pictures do? Look at the pictures and write the correct form of **können** into the gaps. You find the forms in the conjugation box.

1

Wir ______________ sehr gut malen.

2

Melanie und David ______________ tanzen.

3

Du ______________ Klavier spielen.

5 TR. 35

§ 10 Modal verbs

There are 6 modal verbs in German: **können**, **dürfen**, **müssen**, **sollen**, **wollen** and **mögen**.
Modals are usually followed by a second verb in the infinitive form:

David kann malen.	*David can paint.*

The modal verb modifies the meaning of the second verb (infinitive), for example:

Ich kann tanzen.	*I can dance.*
and	
Ich will tanzen.	*I want to dance.*

The infinitive is placed at the very end of the sentence.
You may also listen to these sentences on the CD.

6 TR. 36

dürfen
ich darf
du darfst
er / sie / es darf
wir dürfen
ihr dürft
sie / Sie dürfen

The modal verb **können** (*can*) expresses an ability, a possibility or a request.

Dürfen (*may*) is used to give permission and for polite requests. Read the sentences below and write the correct form of **können** oder **dürfen** into the gap. You find the clues in brackets.

You can also find these sentences on the CD.

1. David ______________ wirklich gut Tango tanzen. (*ability*)
2. Wir ______________ von ihm viel lernen. (*possibility*)
3. David, ______________ du mir helfen? (*request*)
4. ______________ ich mit Ihnen tanzen? (*polite request*)
5. Sie ______________ sehr gerne mit mir tanzen. (*permission*)
6. Tut mir leid, ich ______________ nicht tanzen. (*inability*)

müssen
ich muss
du musst
er / sie / es muss
wir müssen
ihr müsst
sie / Sie müssen

sollen
ich soll
du sollst
er / sie / es soll
wir sollen
ihr sollt
sie / Sie sollen

7

Müssen and **sollen** are used to express duties, obligations or recommendations. It depends on the speaker's point of view which of the two is more appropriate. For example:

Man soll sich dreimal täglich die Zähne putzen.
The speaker thinks that one should brush ones teeth three times a day, but it is only recommendable and not absolutely necessary.

To say: **Man muss sich dreimal täglich die Zähne putzen.** is also correct and makes sense. The difference is that the speaker is convinced that brushing one's teeth 3 times a day is absolutely necessary and has to be done by all means.

The modal verb **müssen** is used to express a necessity.
Sollen expresses a (moral) obligation or even an (indirect) order.

Müssen expresses an obligation or a necessity:

Obligation:

Mein Chef sagt, ich muss am Samstag arbeiten.
My boss says, I have to work on Saturday.

Necessity:

Ich habe großen Hunger – ich muss etwas essen.
I'm very hungry – I have to eat something.

Sollen expresses a moral obligation or an order/advice:

Moral obligation:

Du sollst anderen Menschen helfen.
You shall help other people.

Soll ich dir helfen?
Do you want me to help you?

Sofie hat angerufen, du sollst sie zurück rufen.
Sofie called, you shall call her back.

Advice:

Du sollst nicht so viel rauchen.
You shouldn't smoke so much.

Order:

Du sollst das nicht machen.
Don't do that!

8

Müssen and **sollen** both express duties. Whereas **müssen** refers to (legal) obligations or absolute necessities, **sollen** expresses a (moral) obligation.

Read the sentences and write the correct modal verb into the gap.

1. Man ___________ sich dreimal täglich die Zähne putzen.
2. Viele Erwachsene ___________ 8 Stunden am Tag arbeiten.
3. Kinder ___________ viel lernen.
4. Du ___________ pünktlich sein.
5. Ich ___________ nicht lügen.
6. Du bist ein Spitzensportler und ___________ viel trainieren.
7. Kinder ___________ viel Gemüse essen.

Gut zu wissen

The pronoun **man** is used to make general statements as in *One/you should not drink and drive*. **Man** uses the same verb form as **er / sie / es** (third person singular).

9

The modal verbs **müssen** (*to have to*) and **wollen** (*to want to*) can be looked at as opposites. Whereas **müssen** expresses (legal) obligations or (absolute) necessities, **wollen** is used to express a personal wish, desire or intention. Now read the sentences and decide which translation is correct.

1. Ich will ein Eis essen.
   - a. *I want some ice cream.*
   - b. *I have some ice cream.*
   - c. *I eat some ice cream.*

2. Lisa muss viel lernen.
   - a. *Lisa learns a lot.*
   - b. *Lisa has to learn a lot.*
   - c. *Lisa wants to learn a lot.*

3. Sportler müssen hart trainieren.
   - a. *Sportsmen want to train hard.*
   - b. *Sportsmen have to train hard.*
   - c. *Sportsmen hardly train.*

4. Wir wollen ins Kino gehen.
   - a. *We go to the movies.*
   - b. *We like the movies.*
   - c. *We intend to go to the movies.*

5. Willst du mitkommen?
   - a. *Do you want to come?*
   - b. *Will you go?*
   - c. *Can you come?*

6. Ihr müsst "Kongo" sehen!
   - a. *Don't watch "Kongo"!*
   - b. *You have to see "Kongo"!*
   - c. *You want to see "Kongo"!*

wollen

ich will
du willst
er / sie / es will
wir wollen
ihr wollt
sie / Sie wollen

10 TR. 37

mögen
ich mag
du magst
er / sie / es mag
wir mögen
ihr mögt
sie / Sie mögen

mögen
ich möchte
du möchtest
er / sie / es möchte
wir möchten
ihr möchtet
sie / Sie möchten

The modal verb **mögen** is a bit different than the other modals. It is hardly ever used with a second verb in the infinitive.

Mögen followed by a noun expresses a general like or dislike:

> **Die Simmons mögen Katzen.**
> *The Simmons like cats.*
> **Thomas mag kein Bier.**
> *Thomas doesn't like beer.*

It can also be used for a momentary offer or request:

> **Magst du ein Eis?**
> *Do you want some ice cream?*
> **Ich mag ein Vanilleeis.**
> *I want some vanilla ice cream.*

However, it is much more polite and common to use the subjunctive form of **mögen**, when you are talking about a momentary request or offer:

> **Ich möchte ins Kino gehen.**
> *I would like to go to the movies.*
> **David möchte lieber ein Museum besuchen.**
> *David would rather visit a museum.*

You can also find these sentences on the CD.

11

In these rows of letters, there are hidden sentences that you can use to express your likes and dislikes or to make polite requests. Split the chains of letters so that the sentences are correct.

1. MöchtestdueinenKaffee?

   ____

2. IchmöchtelieberreinenTee.

   ____

3. MelaniemagVanilletee.

   ____

4. IhrmögtFilme.

   ____

5. Möchtestdumitmirtanzen?

   ____

12

Let's take a closer look at the modal verb **sollen**.

sollen
ich soll
du sollst
er / sie / es soll
wir sollen
ihr sollt
sie / Sie sollen

sollen can express:

- moral or social obligation:

  Man soll höflich sein.
  One shall/should be polite. (Though it is not written anywhere, politeness is a social norm.)
  Man soll anderen Menschen helfen.
  You shall/ should help other people. (No one forces you to, but it is a moral obligation.)
- indirect or reported command/order

  Du sollst David anrufen.
  You should call David.
  (He called earlier and asked me to tell you to call him back.)
  Ich soll tanzen lernen.
  I shall/should learn to dance.
  (My girlfriend wants me to learn to dance, because she is crazy about dancing and I can't dance at all.)
  Soll ich dir helfen?
  Do you want me to help you?
  (The question precedes a possible order from another person.)
- advice:

  Man soll Stress vermeiden.
  One should avoid stress. (a simple reasonable advice)

13 TR. 38

Now you know all six modal verbs in German. Try to write the corresponding conjugated form of the modal verbs in brackets into the gaps. These examples are also included on the CD.

1. ich ____________________ (müssen)
2. du ____________________ (dürfen)
3. er ____________________ (wollen)
4. ihr ____________________ (sollen)
5. sie ____________________ (können, plural)
6. ich ____________________ (mögen)
7. ihr ____________________ (können)

14

Lisa and her classmates try to impress each other with their abilities and what they are allowed to do. Look at the pictures and write the missing form of **können** or **dürfen** into the gap.

1. Ich ________________ Fahhrad fahren.

2. Wir ________________ Gitarre spielen.

3. Sonja ________________ bis 21.00 fernsehen.

4. Tom ________________ Spaghetti kochen.

5. Du ________________ viel Eis essen.

15

And what are your duties, wishes, likes or abilities? Now you know all six modal verbs in German. Try to translate the sentences below.

1. *I like horror movies.*
2. *I can play the piano.*
3. *I have to work a lot.*
4. *I like pizza.*
5. *I'd like to drink a coffee.*
6. *I'm allowed to read till 10 pm.*
7. *I shall/should eat more vegetables.*
8. *I want to learn German.*

1

Read the sentences and decide which translation is correct.

1. Ich mag Gemüse.
   - a. *I like vegetables.*
   - b. *I want to eat vegetables.*
   - c. *I would like vegetables.*

2. Ihr mögt Filme.
   - a. *You want to watch a movie now.*
   - b. *You like movies in general.*
   - c. *You want a movie.*

3. Wir wollen mit Melanie einen Kaffee trinken.
   - a. *We like coffee.*
   - b. *We intend to go for a coffee.*
   - c. *We order a coffee.*

4. Ich will eine Pizza Hawaii.
   - a. *I intend to eat a pizza later.*
   - b. *I like Pizza Hawaii.*
   - c. *I want a Pizza Hawaii.*

5. Möchtest du mit mir tanzen?
   - a. *Do you like dancing?*
   - b. *Would you like to dance with me?*
   - c. *Do you want to dance with me?*

6. Ich möchte die Spaghetti Napoli.
   - a. *I like Spaghetti Napoli.*
   - b. *I would like the Spaghetti Napoli.*
   - c. *I want the Spaghetti Napoli.*

2

The words in the following sentences are mixed up. Put the words into the right position in order to get correct sentences.

1. Klavier / du / Kannst / spielen / ?
2. Ich / Eis / ein / möchte / .
3. essen / Susanne / eine / will / Pizza / .
4. Sie / Möchten / mir / mit / tanzen / ?
5. Ich / lernen / will / Deutsch / .
6. helfen / Soll / dir / ich / ?

Gut zu wissen

The verb that accompanies the modal verb goes to the end of the sentence.

müssen** and **sollen

Gut zu wissen

It often depends on the speakers point of view if **sollen** or **müssen** is more appropriate. In **Man soll höflich sein.** one talks about a social norm that can also be neglected. Someone who thinks that politeness is an absolute necessity would say **Man muss höflich sein.**

3

Both **müssen** and **sollen** express a duty or an obligation. Decide which of the two is more appropriate and write the correct form into the gap.

1. Lisa ________________ viel lernen.
2. Meine Freundin sagt, ich ________________ tanzen lernen.
3. Du ________________ bitte Thomas anrufen.
4. David ________________ am Sonntag arbeiten.
5. Man ________________ höflich sein.
6. ________________ ich dir helfen?
7. Man ________________ Stress vermeiden.
8. Sportler ________________ viel trainieren.

4

Complete the sentences below by writing the correct form of the appropriate modal verb into the gaps. In brackets you find a hint about which modal would be best.

1. Susanne ________________ Englisch lernen. (*intention*)
2. Lisa ________________ ihr Zimmer aufräumen. (*duty*)
3. Ich ________________ „Kongo" sehen. (*wish*)
4. ________________ Sie einen Tee? (*polite question*)
5. Melanie und David ________________ Katzen. (*like*)
6. Lisa ________________ bis 21 Uhr lesen. (*permission*)
7. Du ________________ David anrufen. (*indirect order*)
8. Ich ________________ mit Dr. Colani Golf spielen. (*obligation*)
9. David ________________ sehr gut Deutsch sprechen. (*ability*)
10. Thomas ________________ viel Gemüse essen. (*advice*)

1 TR. 39

In this module we take a closer look at the other past tense in German, **das Präteritum**.

§ 17 Past tense

Look at the picture of Paul Kowalski's' 70th birthday. On the left you find sentences describing the party using present tense, a tense you already know. Try to match them with the sentences on the right using past tense. Look carefully at the forms. Can you notice any regularity? You can also listen to the sentences on the CD.

1. Birgit und Peter singen.
2. Lisa isst Kuchen.
3. Ida flirtet.
4. Sylvia fotografiert.
5. Die Gäste tanzen.
6. Die Band spielt Musik.
7. Thomas hält eine Rede.

a. Die Band spielte Musik.
b. Die Gäste tanzten.
c. Thomas hielt eine Rede.
d. Birgit und Peter sangen.
e. Ida flirtete.
f. Sylvia fotografierte.
g. Lisa aß Kuchen.

2

The verbs are in the past tense (**Präteritum**). There are regular and irregular verbs.

Regular past tense forms are for example: **flirtete**, **fotografierte**, **tanzten**, **spielte**.

Irregular past tense forms are: **sangen**, **aß**, **hielt**.

3 TR. 40

Regular verbs form the past tense (**Präteritum**) by putting the past tense marker –**t**- between the stem and the personal ending of the verb.

The personal endings are almost the same as in the present tense. The third person singular (**er**, **sie**, **es**) uses the same form as **ich**.

Du and ihr add an –**e** (-**est**, -**et**) to make the marker -**t** more audible.

Example:

tanzen (*to dance*)

ich tanz-**t-e**	wir tanz-**t-en**
du tanz-**t-est**	ihr tanz-**t-et**
er / sie / es tanz-**t-e**	sie / Sie tanz-**ten**

You can also listen to this example on the CD.

4 TR. 41

Verbs like **leben**, **wohnen**, **arbeiten**, **gratulieren** are all regular verbs. Try to form their past tense forms corresponding to the given personal pronoun.

These examples are also included on the CD.

1. er ____________________ (leben)
2. wir ____________________ (wohnen)
3. sie ____________________ (arbeiten, 3rd person singular)
4. sie ____________________ (gratulieren, 3rd person singular)

5

atmen – *to breathe*

Gut zu wissen

If the stem ends in –**d**, -**t** or –**m**, add another –**e** between the stem and marker –**t** for the sake of pronunciation: **er arbeitete.**

Let's look at another regular verb **atmen**. Try to fill the table below by writing correct conjugated past tense form into the gaps. Look at the **Gut zu wissen** box for a clue.

ich ____________________	wir ____________________
du ____________________	ihr ____________________
er / sie / es ____________________	sie / Sie ____________________

6 TR. 42

Irregular verbs form the past tense by changing the stem vowel.

infinitive	past tense
k**o**mmen	k**a**men
g**e**hen	g**i**ng
essen	**a**ß
h**a**lten	h**ie**lt
tr**i**nken	tr**a**nk

Except for the form of **ich** and **er / sie / es** which do not have a personal ending, add the usual personal ending.
Unfortunately there is no rule to know how the stem vowel changes. It is best to learn the past tense (and the participle) with every new verb you come across.
You may also listen to these examples on the CD.

7

Try to conjugate the verbs given in brackets in the past tense forms.

1. ich ______________________________ (kommen)
2. er ______________________________ (gehen)
3. wir ______________________________ (trinken)
4. wir ______________________________ (halten)
5. sie ______________________________ (essen, 3rd person singular)
6. er ______________________________ (kommen)

Gut zu wissen

As you can see in the example of **gehen** ▸ **ging**, some verbs change slightly more than only the stem vowel. This is due to pronunciation. Try saying **ging** without the **g** at the end ... Nearly impossible, your tongue makes the sound automatically when it drops down - so you might just as well add the letter to the word.

8 TR.43

Gut zu wissen

bringen - brachte
wissen – wusste
rennen - rannte

A few verbs form a mixed past tense by changing the stem vowel like irregular verbs and adding the past tense marker –**t**- in front of the personal ending like regular verbs.

For example:

kennen (*to know*)

ich k**a**nn**t**e	wir k**a**nn**t**en
du k**a**nn**t**est	ihr k**a**nn**t**et
er / sie / es k**a**nn**t**e	sie / Sie k**a**nn**t**en

This example is also included on the CD.

Other verbs that form a mixed past tense are: **bringen** (*to bring*), **wissen** (*to know*), **rennen** (*to run*). Look at the **Gut zu wissen** box for their forms.

9 TR. 44

Gut zu wissen

Mitbringen is a separable verb. As in the present tense, the prefix is separated from the stem and goes to the end of the sentence.

Now try to write the correct form of the verbs in brackets into the gap. You can also check the answers listening to the CD.

1. Die Gäste ________________ Geschenke mit. (bringen)
2. Paul ________________ nicht, was er sagen sollte. (wissen)
3. Ich ________________ nicht alle Gäste. (kennen)
4. Viele Kinder ________________ durch den Saal. (rennen)

10

Gut zu wissen

The past tense of **sein** and **haben** is used in the written and the spoken language for all persons. Other verbs rarely use the past tense for **du** and **ihr** - **du gratuliertest** for example sounds rather poetic and old fashioned.

And what about the verbs **sein** (*to be*) and **haben** (*to have*)? The past tense of these two verbs is completely irregular. Look at the table below and try to memorize these forms. It's not so difficult as all you need is the stem of the past form and just add the normal ending.

	haben	sein
ich	ha**tt**e	**war**
du	ha**tt**est	**war**st
er / sie / es	ha**tt**e	**war**
wir	ha**tt**en	**war**en
ihr	ha**tt**et	**war**t
sie / Sie	ha**tt**en	**war**en

11

You saw Paul's niece Ida flirt with someone at his birthday party. Now read about her struggle to become a doctor. Match the sentences to their translation.

1. Ida wollte Arzt werden.
2. Mädchen konnten früher selten studieren.
3. Sie sollten Hausfrau und Mutter sein.
4. Idas Eltern waren sehr modern.
5. Sie mochten keine Regeln.
6. Sie wollten eine glückliche Tochter.
7. Ida durfte die Universität besuchen.
8. Sie konnte studieren.
9. Ida musste viel lernen.
10. Sie wurde eine gute Kinderärztin.

a. They didn't like rules.
b. She could study.
c. Ida's parents were very progressive.
d. In the past girls were rarely able to study at University.
e. She became a good paediatrician.
f. Ida had to learn a lot.
g. Ida wanted to become a doctor.
h. They should be housewives and mothers.
i. They wanted a happy daughter.
j. Ida was allowed to go to university.

12

Let's look at the modal verbs now. They form a regular past tense with the past tense marker -**t**- and the personal endings.

If the infinitive has an umlaut it is lost in the past tense.

können (*can*) ▸ **sie konnte** (*she could*)

However there is one exception to this rule. Look at the modal verb **mögen** (*to like*).

ich mo**ch**te	wir mo**ch**ten
du mo**ch**test	ihr mo**ch**tet
er / sie / es mo**ch**te	sie / Sie mo**ch**ten

Gut zu wissen

As with **sein** and **haben**, the past tense of modal verbs is also used in spoken and written German with each personal pronoun.

13

Gut zu wissen

If the infinitive has an umlaut it is lost in the past tense.

It's your turn now! Try to fill in the gaps with the correct past form of the modal verbs **können** und **dürfen**.

	können	dürfen
ich	________________	________________
du	________________	________________
er / sie / es	________________	durfte
wir	konnten	________________
ihr	________________	durftet
sie / Sie	________________	________________

14 TR. 45

§ 2 Adverbs

Let's go back to Paul's birthday party. He really enjoyed it and wrote about it in his diary. Read the sentences together with the translation. You also find these sentences on the CD.

Gut zu wissen

heute, **zuerst**, **dann**, **immer**, **danach**, **früher**, **jetzt** and **nie** are adverbs of time or frequency.

Heute war ein toller Tag.
Today was a great day.

Zuerst gratulierte mir der Bürgermeister.
First the mayor congratulated me.

Dann hielt Thomas eine Rede.
Then Thomas made a speech.

Er spricht **immer** sehr gut.
Lit: He always speaks very well.

Danach sangen Birgit und Pierre ein Geburtstagslied.
After that Birgit and Pierre sang a birthday song.

Dann gab es Essen.
Then we had dinner.

Und **dann** tanzten und feierten wir.
And then we danced and celebrated.

Früher wollte ich nie alt sein.
I never wanted to be old.

Jetzt bin ich 70.
Now I am 70 years old.

Und ich war **nie** so glücklich.
And I was never happier.

15

Paul wrote in his diary for example:

§ 2 Adverbs

> **Früher** wollte ich nie alt sein.
> **Heute** bin ich 70.
> Ich war **nie** so glücklich.

The bold words are adverbs, i.e. expressions of time (then, afterwards, etc.) or frequency (always, sometimes, ...) that give further information about a verb, i.e. when or how frequently something is done. Adverbs of frequency are usually placed behind the conjugated verb.

Adverbs of time can also be placed at the beginning of the sentence.

Note that with an adverb at the beginning of the sentence the position of verb and subject changes.

Normal word order:	**Ich bin 70.**
With adverb:	**Heute bin ich 70.**

16

Now try to match the German adverbs with their English translation.

Gut zu wissen

Adverbs do not change, regardless of the case, the tense, the article: adverbs stay the same.

today - always - earlier - now - never - first - after that - seldom - then

1. heute ____________
2. zuerst ____________
3. dann ____________
4. immer ____________
5. danach ____________
6. früher ____________
7. jetzt ____________
8. nie ____________
9. selten ____________

17 TR. 46

The sentences in Paul's diary got mixed up. Try to put the words into the right order and create a correct sentence describing his birthday party. Look at the pictures for a clue.

1. Zuerst / der Bürgermeister / gratulierte / .

____

2. Thomas / Rede / hielt / eine / Dann / .

____

3. Birgit und Pierre / Danach / ein Geburtstagslied / sangen / .

____

4. gab / es / Dann / Essen / .

____

5. und / tanzten / wir / dann / feierten / Und / .

____

6. noch / so / Ich / glücklich / war / nie / .

____

1

Read the sentences and decide which answer is correct.

1. To form the past tense of regular verbs
   - a. change the stem vowel.
   - b. add –**t** to the stem.
   - c. add a past tense ending.

2. To form the past tense of irregular verbs
   - a. add –**t** to the stem.
   - b. add a past tense ending.
   - c. change the stem vowel.

3. The past tense of **können** is
   - a. **konnte**.
   - b. **könnte**.
   - c. **kannte**.

4. Separable verbs in the past tense
   - a. hold on to the prefix.
   - b. send the prefix to the end of the sentence.
   - c. do not form a past tense.

5. The past tense is mostly
   - a. used in spoken German.
   - b. used in written and spoken German.
   - c. used in written German.

6. The past tense of **sein**, **haben** and the modals
   - a. is used in spoken German.
   - b. is used in written German.
   - c. is used in spoken and written German.

2

Try to fill in the gaps with the correct past form of the modal verbs **müssen** and **sollen**.

	müssen	sollen
ich	____________	____________
du	____________	____________
er / sie / es	____________	sollte
wir	mussten	____________
ihr	____________	solltet
sie / Sie	____________	____________

past tense - adverbs

3

werden
ich wurde
du wurdest
er / sie / es wurde
wir wurden
ihr wurdet
sie / Sie wurden

Complete the sentences by writing the correct past tense form of the infinitives in brackets.

1. Idas Eltern _______________ sehr modern. (sein)
2. Mädchen _______________ früher selten studieren. (können)
3. Sie _______________ eine gute Kinderärztin. (werden)
4. Lisa _______________ zu viel Kuchen. (essen)
5. Der Bürgermeister _______________ Paul. (gratulieren)
6. Der Bürgermeister _______________ erst spät. (gehen)
7. Die Gäste _______________ Geschenke _______________. (mitbringen)
8. Viele Kinder _______________ durch den Saal. (rennen)
9. Die Gäste _______________. (tanzen)
10. Sylvia _______________ die Gäste. (fotografieren)
11. Die Band _______________ gute Musik. (spielen)
12. Ida _______________ die Universität besuchen. (dürfen)

4 TR. 47

oft – *often*
nie – *never*
selten – *rarely*
immer – *always*
manchmal – *sometimes*
früher – *previously*
heute – *today*
jetzt – *now*
nachher – *later*
morgen – *tomorrow*
dann - *then*

Below you find some more adverbs. Which of them give information about frequency and which about time? Check the word box for the translation and then write them into the correct box. You can also listen to these adverbs on the CD.

nachher - nie - dann - immer - manchmal - früher - jetzt - oft - heute - selten - morgen

frequency	time

1 TR. 48

What to wear? Look at the pictures and the **Gut zu wissen** box and try to memorize the words together with the corresponding article.

All these words are also included on the CD.

1. **die Jacke** - *jacket*
2. **der Anzug** - *suit*
3. **das Hemd** - *shirt*
4. **die Schuhe** - *shoes*
5. **der Rock** - *skirt*
6. **die Strümpfe** - *socks*
7. **die Hose** - *trousers*
8. **der Pullover** - *jumper*
9. **das Kleid** - *dress*
10. **das T-Shirt** - *T-shirt*

Gut zu wissen

Die Strümpfe (*socks*) and **die Schuhe** (*shoes*) are plural because they usually go in pairs. **der Strumpf**, **der Schuh** are the singular words. *Clothes* in general are: **die Kleidung** (singular, even though the idea is plural) or **die Kleider.**

2

As you already know, there are definite (**der**, **die**, **das**) and indefinite (**ein**, **eine**) articles in German. Their forms depend on the gender, the case and the number of the corresponding noun.

Now fill in the tables below with the appropriate form of the article.

singular	masculine	feminine	neuter
nom.	der	die	das
acc.	___________	___________	___________

plural	all genders
nom.	die
acc.	___________

singular	masculine	feminine	neuter
nom.	ein	eine	ein
acc.	___________	___________	___________

§ 3 Article - definitive

§ 4 Article - indefinitive

Gut zu wissen

The indefinite article has no plural form.

3 TR. 49

In this module we deal with adjectives.

Read the German sentences below and try to match them with the English translation.

You can also listen to theses example on the CD.

1. Die Hose ist bequem.
2. Lisa hat ein rotes Kleid.
3. Der Anzug ist am teuersten.
4. Thomas ist älter als Susanne.
5. Ich trage einen langen Rock.

a. Thomas is older than Susanne.
b. I'm wearing a long skirt.
c. The trousers are comfortable.
d. The suit is the most expensive.
e. Lisa has a red dress.

4 TR. 50

schön – *beautiful*
verrückt – *crazy*
teuer – *expensive*
modern – *fashionable*
alt – *old*
kurz - *short*

Adjectives describe how someone or something is. After a form of **sein**, adjectives are used in their basic form, i.e. without ending. The same form is used for all gender and in both the singular and plural.

Try to translate the following sentences into German. You find the necessary adjectives in the word box on the left.

These examples are also included on the CD.

1. *You are beautiful.*

   ____

2. *Life is crazy.*

   ____

3. *The clothes are expensive.*

   ____

4. *Skirts were fashionable.*

   ____

5. *Paul is old.*

   ____

6. *The skirt was short.*

   ____

5 TR. 51

Susanne, Melanie and Thomas are watching a fashion show on TV. Read the dialogue. You may also listen to it on the CD.

Susanne: Seht mal ... Der grüne Rock und die rote Jacke.
Melanie: Die sind hässlich!
Susanne: Und das kurze T-Shirt dazu. Ein normaler Mensch zieht das nicht an.
Thomas: Das ist auch eine Modenschau und nicht das normale Leben.
Melanie: Die Modelle sind auch nicht normal.
Susanne: Das ist richtig. Eine normale Frau ist dicker als ein Modell.
Melanie: Und kleiner.
Susanne: Du bist groß.
Melanie: Ja, ich bin größer als der Durchschnitt, aber nicht so groß wie ein Modell. Meine Beine sind definitiv kürzer - und meine Röcke sind länger.
Susanne: Modelle haben immer so lange Beine. Ich habe gelesen, die Beine von Nadja Auermann sind am längsten.
Melanie: Wer ist Nadja Auermann?
Susanne: Ein berühmtes deutsches Fotomodell.
Thomas: Seht mal. Das helle Kleid ist sehr schön.
Melanie: Ja, ein schönes Kleid. Aber eine helle Farbe ist nicht praktisch.
Thomas: Die Kleidung in einer Modenschau ist fast nie praktisch. Sie ist modern und teuer. Die verrückten Kleider kann man ansehen, aber man trägt sie nicht.
Susanne: Ich finde, Hosen sind sowieso praktischer als Kleider und viel bequemer.
Thomas: Oh ja, das ist richtig.
Melanie: Woher weißt du das? Du trägst täglich einen bequemen Anzug.
Thomas: Ja, aber ich hatte auch einen grünen Rock.
Melanie: Ja, ja. Und eine rote Jacke. Und ein kurzes T-Shirt dazu.
Thomas: Doch, das ist wahr. Röcke für Männer waren total modern. Von allen Männern in Düsseldorf war ich am schönsten.
Melanie: Du bist ja verrückt!
Susanne: Nein, Thomas ist nur besonders lustig heute. Er hatte keinen Rock.
Thomas: Ja, leider. Ein kurzer Rock ist mein Traum, aber meine Beine sind einfach zu dünn.

§ 5 Comparision

Komparativ

Adjektiv + -er

Superlativ

am + Adjektiv + -sten

hoch höher am höchsten

nah näher am nächsten

gut besser am besten

viel mehr am meisten

6

Adjectives can be used in a comparative sense.
For example:

Thomas ist klein.	*Thomas is small.*
Susanne ist kleiner.	*Susanne is smaller.*
Lisa ist am kleinsten.	*Lisa is the smallest.*

klein is the basic form, **kleiner** is the comparative and **am kleinsten** is the superlative.
One-syllable adjectives often take an umlaut in the comparative and superlative.
For example:

a ▸ **ä**

alt (*old*) — **älter** (*o/elder*) — **am ältesten** (*o/eldest*)

u ▸ **ü**

jung (*young*) — **jünger** (*younger*) — **am jüngsten** (*youngest*)

o ▸ **ö**

groß (*big*) — **größer** (*bigger*) — **am größten** (*biggest*)

The superlative of adjectives that end in –**d**, –**t**, –**s**, –**sch** and –**z** take the ending –**esten.**
For example: **am ältesten**, **am kürzesten**

7 TR. 52

Now try to fill in the table below with the correct form of the given adjectives in brackets.

You can also listen to these adjectives on the CD.

basic form	comparative	superlative
schön	______________	______________
lang	______________	______________

8

With the words **zu** and **sehr** you can stress an adjective.

zu + basic adjective:
Das Leben ist **zu** kurz.
*Life is **too** short.*

sehr + adjective:
Du bist **sehr** schön.
*You are **very** beautiful.*

With **nicht** you negate an adjective.

nicht + adjective:
Das ist **nicht** gut.
*That's **not** good.*

9

§ 1 Adjectives

Adjectives that describe a noun and that appear directly before the noun change their ending. The adjectival ending depends on the gender, the plurality, the case and whether the article that accompanies the noun is definite or indefinite.

When the noun is accompanied by a definite article (**der**, **die**, **das**) the adjective takes the following endings:

	masculine	feminine	neuter
nominative	der schön**e** Rock	die schön**e** Jacke	das schön**e** Kleid
accusative	den schön**en** Rock	die schön**e** Jacke	das schön**e** Kleid

The plural (**die**) takes the ending –**en** in all cases.

Die schön**en** Schuhe.

10 TR. 53

Try to write the correct form of the adjective in brackets into the gap. You can also listen to these examples on the CD.

1. der ____________ Pullover (grün)
2. die ____________ Jacke (rot)
3. das ____________ Kleid (hell)
4. den ____________ Rock (kurz)
5. die ____________ Hose (bequem)

1. the green pullover
2. the red jacket
3. the light-coloured dress
4. the short skirt
5. the comfortable trousers

11

Someone gave you 500 Euros to spend on clothes. What do you buy? The given nouns are in the nominative case. Write the correct sentences putting the nouns into the accusative case. Start with:

Ich kaufe … (*I buy* …)

1. die verrückten Schuhe ____________
2. der schöne Rock ____________
3. die praktische Hose ____________
4. der teure Anzug ____________
5. das grüne Hemd ____________

adjectives with the indefinite article

12

§ 1 Adjectives

When the noun is accompanied by an indefinite article (**ein**, **eine**), the adjective takes the following endings:

	masculine	feminine	neuter
nominative	ein schön**er** Rock	eine schön**e** Hose	ein schön**es** Hemd
accusative	einen schön**en** Rock	eine schön**e** Hose	ein schön**es** Hemd

There is no plural for the indefinite article.

13

TR.54

Gut zu wissen

tragen (*to carry*) in combination with clothes means to wear.
Er trägt einen Anzug.
He wears a suit.
Er hat einen Anzug an, also means *to wear*.
The separable verb **anziehen** means *to put on*:
Sie zieht eine Hose an.

Now write the correct form of the adjective into the gap.
You also find these sentences on the CD.

1. Thomas ist ein __________________ Mensch. (normal)
2. Er trägt einen __________________ Anzug. (bequem)
3. Lisa hat eine __________________ Hose an. (kurz)
4. Susanne zieht ein __________________ Kleid an. (schön)

14

Look at the pictures and read the sentences below. Mark the sentence that matches the picture.

- a. Sie zieht eine lange Jacke an.
- b. Sie zieht ein langes T-shirt an.
- c. Sie zieht ein langes Kleid an.

- a. Thomas trägt oft eine kurze Hose.
- b. Thomas trägt oft einen kurzen Rock.
- c. Thomas trägt oft ein kurzes Kleid.

15

§ 5 Comparison

The construction: **so** + adjective + **wie** expresses that two things / people are the same.

Susanne ist **so** groß **wie** der Durchschnitt.
Susanne is as tall as the average.

fast so + adjective + **wie** expresses that two things / people are almost the same.

Melanie ist **fast so** groß **wie** Thomas.
Melanie is almost as tall as Thomas.

genauso + adjective + **wie** expresses that two things / people are exactly the same.

Der Rock ist **genauso** teuer **wie** das T-Shirt.
The skirt is exactly as expensive as the T-shirt.

When two things / people are different use: comparative + **als**.

Susanne ist dicker **als** Melanie.

16

Read the following comparisons and try to match them to their correct translation.

1. Die Frau ist kleiner als der Mann.
2. Der Rock ist genauso teuer wie das T-Shirt.
3. Susanne ist dicker als Melanie.
4. Die Hose ist bequemer als das Kleid.
5. Susanne ist so groß wie der Durchschnitt.
6. Melanies Röcke sind länger als Anjas.
7. Eine dunkle Farbe ist praktischer als eine helle Farbe.
8. Die Modenschau ist verrückter als das normale Leben.
9. Melanie ist fast so groß wie Thomas.

a. A dark colour is more practical than a light colour.
b. Susanne is as tall as the average.
c. The woman is smaller than the man.
d. Melanie is almost as tall as Thomas.
e. The fashion show is crazier than normal life.
f. The skirt is as expensive as the T-shirt.
g. Susanne is bigger than Melanie.
h. Melanies skirts are longer than Anjas.
i. The trousers are more comfortable than the dress.

Gut zu wissen

Adjectives that come after the verb form of **sein** don't have an ending.
Adjectives in front of a noun change their ending according to the case, gender, plurality and the type of article.

17

Look at the picture and write the correct form of the adjective in brackets.

1. Die Frau trägt einen ___________ (rot) Rock und eine ___________ (lang) Jacke.
2. Die Schuhe sind ___________ (neu).
3. Der Mann hat ein ___________ (grün) Hemd an.
4. Die Hose ist zu ___________ (groß).
5. Das Kind trägt ein ___________ (kurz) T-Shirt und eine ___________ (lang) Hose.
6. Die Hosen sind sehr ___________ (bequem).

18

The words in the following comparison sentences are mixed up.
Put them into correct order.

1. größer / Melanie / der Durchschnitt / ist / als / .

   ____

2. teuer / das T-Shirt/ so / Der Rock / ist / wie / .

   ____

3. als / praktischer / ist / Eine Hose / ein Kleid / .

   ____

4. verrückt / ist / Das Leben / wie / eine Modenschau / so / .

   ____

5. Lisa / so / ist / groß / fast / wie / Susanne / .

   ____

6. Ein grünes / schöner / Hemd / als / Pullover / ist / ein roter / .

   ____

7. bequemer / Die lange / ist / Hose / .

   ____

adjectives

1

Look at the pictures and read the sentences below. Mark the sentence that matches the picture.

1

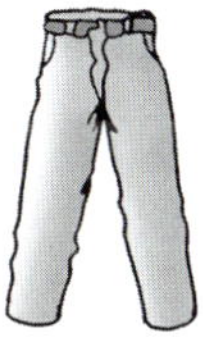

- ■ a. Ich möchte eine moderne Hose.
- ■ b. Ich möchte einen modernen Rock.
- ■ c. Ich möchte ein modernes T-Shirt.

2

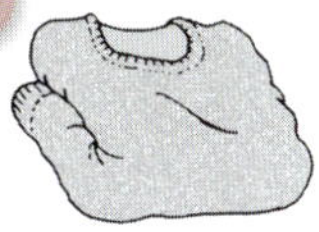

- ■ a. David hat einen teuren Pullover an.
- ■ b. David hat eine teure Jacke an.
- ■ c. David hat ein teures Hemd an

3

- ■ a. Haben Sie einen roten Pullover?
- ■ b. Haben Sie eine rote Jacke?
- ■ c. Haben Sie ein rotes T-shirt?

Gut zu wissen

Some adjectives like **teuer** (*expensive*), lose an **-e** when declinated: **teuer – teure, teures, teuren.**

2

What are you wearing now? The given nouns are in the nominative case. Write the correct sentences putting the nouns into the accusative case. Start with:

Ich trage ... (*I wear ...*)

1. die langen Strümpfe

___

2. der gute Pullover

___

3. das kurze Kleid

___

4. das große T-Shirt

___

5. die rote Jacke

___

comparison

3

Write the comparative and superlative forms of the given adjectives.

basic	*comparative*	*superlative*
1. groß	______________	______________
2. praktisch	______________	______________
3. berühmt	______________	______________
4. teuer	______________	______________
5. modern	______________	______________
6. gut	______________	______________
7. kurz	______________	______________
8. alt	______________	______________

4

The following comparisons are incomplete. Decide whether **wie** or **als** is missing and write the correct form into the gap.

1. Melanie ist größer ____________ der Durchschnitt.
2. Der Rock ist so teuer ____________ das T-Shirt.
3. Eine Hose ist praktischer ____________ ein Kleid.
4. Das Hemd ist so modern ____________ das T-Shirt.
5. Lisa ist fast so groß ____________ Susanne.
6. Das grüne Hemd ist schöner ____________ das rote T-Shirt.
7. Die lange Hose ist so bequem____________ die kurze Hose.
8. Die Modenschau ist verrückter ____________ das normale Leben.

1 TR. 55

Susanne finds an anonymous letter on the stairway. She wonders whose it may be and asks everyone in the house. Match the sentences on the right hand side to the correct person on the left. You may also listen to these sentences on the CD.

1. ich	a. Ist das **ihr** Brief?
2. du	b. Ist das **euer** Brief?
3. er	c. Ist das **unser** Brief?
4. sie	d. Ist das **mein** Brief?
5. es	e. Ist das **Ihr** Brief, Frau Beck?
6. wir	f. Ist das **sein** Brief?
7. ihr	g. Ist das **dein** Brief?
8. Sie	h. Ist das **sein** Brief?

2

You already know the personal pronouns in the nominative case on the left hand side. The bold words on the right are possessive pronouns in the nominative case.

§ 20 Possessive pronouns

personal pronoun	possesive pronoun
ich (*I*)	**mein** (*my*)
du (*you*)	**dein** (*your*)
er (*he*)	**sein** (*his*)
sie (*she*)	**ihr** (*her*)
es (*it*)	**sein** (*its*)
wir (*we*)	**unser** (*our*)
ihr (*you*)	**euer** (*your, informal*)
sie (*they*)	**ihr** (*their*)
Sie (*you, polite*)	**Ihr** (*your, polite*)

3

The possessive pronouns in the table above are without their endings. They are the same as those of **ein**. To add the correct ending you have to look at the gender, the case and the number of the noun.

ein Mann
eine Frau
ein Kind

Try to write the missing ending in the gaps. All nouns are in the nominative case. Look at the word box for a clue.

1. mein_______ Tante
2. dein_______ Nachbarin
3. unser_______ Onkel

4 TR. 56

Susanne is having her evening off today. Read the dialogue below paying special attention to the pronouns appearing in the conversation.

You may also listen to this dialogue while reading.

Thomas: Hallo mein Schatz, ich bin zu Hause.

Susanne: Super. Dann komm bitte gleich in die Küche.

Thomas: Meine fleißige Frau hat gekocht und das Essen wartet auf mich, richtig? Was gibt es heute?

Susanne: Heute gibt es: Thomas kocht das Abendessen für sich und für seine Tochter.

Thomas: Was?

Susanne: Mein lieber Mann hat etwas vergessen: seine Frau hat heute ihren freien Abend.

Thomas: Oh nein ..., das habe ich total vergessen.

Susanne: Dein Gedächtnis ist wirklich sehr schlecht, Thomas! Wie spät ist es?

Thomas: Es ist fast sieben Uhr.

Susanne: Ich muss mich jetzt beeilen. Ich muss mich noch duschen und mich anziehen.

Thomas: Was machst du heute Abend?

Susanne: Ich treffe mich mit meinen Freundinnen. Wir besuchen eine Kunstausstellung.

Thomas: Ich interessiere mich auch für Kunst.

Susanne: Ich weiß, mein Lieber. Es ist auch sehr schade, dass du nicht mitkommst. Aber heute Abend ist Frauenabend, es tut mir Leid. Und jetzt muss ich mich wirklich beeilen. Lisa? Lisa, heute kocht der Papa dein Essen. Was hältst du von deiner Lieblingspizza vom Italiener?

Lisa: Oh ja, lecker.

Thomas: Gut, dann rufe ich mal unseren Freund Giovanni an.

Susanne: So, Lisa, ich gehe jetzt. Wo ist dein Vater?

Lisa: Mein Vater kocht gerade mit seinem Freund Giovanni das Essen.

Thomas: Genau. Unsere Pizza ist in 20 Minuten fertig.

Susanne: Na dann: Guten Appetit! Langweilt euch nicht ohne mich.

Thomas: Keine Sorge, wir können uns beschäftigen. Hier ist deine Jacke.

Susanne: Ich danke dir. Tschüss, meine Süßen.

Thomas: Tschüss. Und amüsiert euch gut!

Amüsiert euch gut!
– Enjoy yourselves!

5

Read the sentences on the left and match them with the correct translation. Read again and pay special attention to the possessive pronouns.

1. Susanne freut sich auf ihren freien Abend.
2. Thomas und seine Tochter bleiben zu Hause.
3. Du triffst deine Freundinnen.
4. Wir bestellen unsere Lieblingspizza.
5. Ihr seht euren Film.
6. Das Kind liest sein Buch.
7. Ich koche mein Essen.
8. Ihr besucht euren Nachbarn.

a. The child reads its book.
b. We order our favorite pizza.
c. You visit your neighbour.
d. Thomas and his daughter stay at home.
e. You meet your girlfriends.
f. Susanne is looking forward to her evening off.
g. You watch your movie.
h. I cook my food.

6

§ 20 Possessive pronouns

Possessive pronouns change their ending according to the gender of the noun they accompany and according to the case of the noun. The possessive pronouns in the sentences of this exercise are all in the accusative case. The endings are as follows:

masculine	feminine	neuter
mein**en**	mein**e**	mein
dein**en**	dein**e**	dein
sein**en**	sein**e**	sein
ihr**en**	ihr**e**	ihr
sein**en**	sein**e**	sein
unser**en**	unser**e**	unser
eur**en**	**eure**	euer
ihr**en** / Ihr**en**	ihr**e** / Ihr**e**	ihr / Ihr

In the accusative plural the possessive pronouns add an –**e**.

possessive pronouns in the dative case

7

▶ § 20 Possessive pronouns

The possessive pronouns also exist in the dative case.
In the singular, the possessive pronouns add the same endings as the indefinite article:

masculine: mein**em** Freund
feminine: mein**er** Freundin
neuter: mein**em** Kind

In the plural the dative possessive pronouns add –**en**:

mein**en** Freunden
mein**en** Kindern

8 TR. 57

Gut zu wissen

Watch out for the use in the 3rd person singular. The pronoun **sein** (*his*) refers to a male or neuter owner and **ihr** (*her*) to a female owner.

Read the sentences and write the correct possessive pronoun in the dative case into the gap.

You can also listen to these sentences on the CD.

1. Er telefoniert mit ____________ Freund Giovanni.
2. Er bedankt sich bei ____________ Frau.
3. Sie hilft ____________ Kind.
4. Sie trifft sich mit ____________ Freunden.

9

Gut zu wissen

Note that the pronoun **euer** (*your, plural*) drops the –**e** before the –**r** when declinated: **eurer** Tochter, **eurem** Nachbarn.
Exception: **euer** - used with neuter nouns- does not drop the –**e**: **euer** Kind.

Read the incomplete sentences on top of each table. Decide which of the possessive pronouns (plus item) completes the sentence and write them into the correct table.

Ich sehe ...	Ich spreche mit ...

seinen Vater - ihre Tochter - euer Kind - unserem Freund - deiner Mutter - seinem Vater - eure Tochter - deine Mutter - ihrer Tochter - unseren Freund - eurem Nachbarn - eurer Tochter

10 TR. 58

Look at the picture and read the German verbs below. Try to match them with the English translation. You can also listen to these verbs and practice your pronunciation.

1. frühstücken	*a. to amuse oneself*
2. sich duschen	*b. to get dressed*
3. sich rasieren	*c. to meet*
4. telefonieren	*d. to say sorry*
5. sich anziehen	*e. to have a shower*
6. sich entschuldigen	*f. to shave*
7. sich treffen	*g. to be late*
8. essen	*h. to phone*
9. sich amüsieren	*i. to have breakfast*
10. sich verspäten	*j. to eat*

11

§ 23 Reflexive verbs

Some verbs in the exercise above are reflexive. Reflexive verbs express that the subject which carries out the action and the person/thing which is affected by the action (the object) are identical. The marker for the infinitive of a reflexive verb is the pronoun **sich** (*oneself*).

sich amüsieren — *to amuse oneself*
Susanne amüsiert **sich**.

sich rasieren — *to shave*
Thomas rasiert **sich**. — *Thomas shaves (himself.)*

Take a closer look at the table with reflexive pronouns.

personal pronoun	reflexive pronoun
ich	mich
du	dich
er / sie / es	sich
wir	uns
ihr	euch
sie / Sie	sich

12 TR. 59

1. I'm getting dressed.
2. You are looking forward to the evening.
3. The child says sorry.
4. We agree to meet at the café.
5. You'll meet each other this evening.
6. They are interested in art.

Read the sentence and write the missing reflexive pronoun into the gap. In the word box you'll find the translation of these sentences.

The German sentences are also included on the CD.

1. Ich ziehe ____________ an.
2. Du freust ____________ auf den Abend.
3. Das Kind entschuldigt ____________.
4. Wir verabreden ____________ im Café.
5. Ihr trefft ____________ heute Abend.
6. Susanne und Melanie interessieren ____________ für Kunst.

13 TR. 60

▶ § 19 Personal pronouns

Personal pronouns are used to substitute a noun in the sentence. The personal pronoun changes according to the case. Read the following examples. They are also included on the CD.

Nominative	Accusative	Dative
ich	Melanie ruft **mich** an.	Melanie dankt **mir**.
er	Du rufst **ihn** an.	Du dankst **ihm**.
Sie	Ich rufe **Sie** an.	Ich danke **Ihnen**.
wir	Er ruft **uns** an.	Er dankt **uns**.

14 TR. 61

It's very good to know all the different pronouns. But it is even better to pronounce them correctly. Here are some pronunciation tips:

For the **ch**-sound after **i**, position your tongue as if you wanted to say yes, smile a little and then breathe out. **Ich**....... And remember that the **i**-sound is short.

An -**r** at the end of a word almost always sounds like a German **a**: dia (**dir**).

In general: make sure to carefully pronounce the ending of the pronoun since it carries important information. (**ihn** / **ihm**)

You may now listen to the examples on the CD and repeat them paying special attention to the correct pronounciation.

15

Substitute the words in brackets with the correct accusative pronoun. Look at the word box for a clue.

mich
dich
ihn / sie / es
uns
euch
sie / Sie

1. Die Frau liest ____________. (das Buch)
2. Thomas sieht ____________ heute Abend. (ihr)
3. Wir bestellen ____________ bei Giovanni. (die Pizza)
4. Ich rufe ____________ an. (Giovanni)
5. Wir treffen ____________ im Café. (unsere Nachbarn)
6. Du besuchst ____________ morgen. (ich)
7. Ich freue mich auf ____________. (du)
8. Besucht ihr ____________ heute? (wir)

16

Complete the *thank you* lines by writing the correct dative pronoun into the gap. The (nominative) pronoun in brackets will give you a clue.

1. Ich danke (du) ____________ für die Pizza.
2. Wir danken (Sie) ____________ für den Abend.
3. Du musst (ich) ____________ nicht danken.
4. Er dankt (wir) ____________ für unseren Besuch.
5. Susanne dankt (er) ____________ für die Blumen.
6. Melanie dankt (sie, singular) ____________ für den Kaffee.
7. Ich danke (ihr) ____________ für eure Hilfe.
8. Sie dankt (sie, plural) ____________ für die Einladung.

17

The personal pronoun **es** can be used to substitute a neuter noun.

Ich lese **ein Buch**. **Es** ist gut.
I read a book. It is good.

Very often the pronoun **es** is used as a formal subject in sentences where there is no other subject:

Es ist spät.	*It is late.*
Es tut mir leid.	*I am sorry.*
Wie geht **es** dir?	*How is it going? / How are you?*
Es geht mir gut.	*It is going ok. / I am fine.*

18

In sentences with reflexive pronouns the subject and the direct object of the sentence are the same person.

reflexive:

Du rasierst dich.	*You shave yourself.* (One person)
Ihr langweilt euch.	*You are bored.*

not reflexive:

Sie rasiert ihn.	*She shaves him.* (Two persons)
Ihr langweilt mich.	*You bore me.*

In some cases the same verb can be reflexive or not:

Er trifft ihn.	*He meets him.* (Two different masculine people.)
Sie trifft sich mit ihm.	*She meets (herself) with him.*

19

Read the sentences. Mark the ones that use reflexive verbs.

1. ☐ Er sieht ihn.
2. ☐ Ich treffe mich mit ihm.
3. ☐ Du rasierst dich.
4. ☐ Sie rasiert ihn.
5. ☐ Wir beeilen uns.
6. ☐ Er freut sich.
7. ☐ Ihr langweilt mich.
8. ☐ Ihr langweilt euch.

20

Write the correct reflexive pronoun into the gap.

1. Ich ziehe ______________ an.
2. Er trifft ______________ mit Thomas.
3. Wir beeilen ______________.
4. Susanne muss ______________ duschen.
5. Ihr freut ______________ auf den Abend.
6. Sie bedanken ______________ für die Blumen.
7. Du entschuldigst ______________.

1

Read the following two words. The owner is the first word and the possession is the second word. Then mark in the box in front of the correct sentence that uses the correct possessive pronoun.

1. Thomas, die Tochter
   - ■ a. Lisa ist seine Tochter.
   - ■ b. Lisa ist meine Tochter.
   - ■ c. Lisa ist ihre Tochter.

2. ich, der Mann
   - ■ a. Ich sehe seinen Mann.
   - ■ b. Ich sehe deinen Mann.
   - ■ c. Er sieht meinen Mann.

3. Susanne, die Freunde
   - ■ a. Sie trifft sich mit ihren Freunden.
   - ■ b. Sie trifft sich mit seinen Freunden.
   - ■ c. Sie treffen meine Freunde.

4. Wir, das Buch
   - ■ a. Wir lesen euer Buch.
   - ■ b. Wir lesen unser Buch.
   - ■ c. Ihr lest euer Buch.

5. Ihr, das Essen
   - ■ a. Ich koche unser Essen.
   - ■ b. Ich koche euer Essen.
   - ■ c. Ihr esst euere Pizza.

6. Sie, der Brief
   - ■ a. Ist das ihr Brief?
   - ■ b. Ist das sein Brief?
   - ■ c. Ist das Ihr Brief?

2

Choose the correct pronoun to complete the sentences.

1. Ich ziehe *mich* / *mir* / *mein* an.
2. Amüsiert *ihr* / *euch* / *euer* gut.
3. Ist das *Ihr* / *ihren* / *sich* Brief?
4. Wir besuchen *dich* / *dir* / *du* morgen.
5. Lisa ist *sein* / *seine* / *ihr* Tochter.
6. Ich bestelle *uns* / *unsere* / *mich* Lieblingspizza.
7. Thomas trifft *euer* / *ihr*/ *euch* im Café.

personal pronouns

3

Mark the pronoun that substitutes the person / thing in brackets.

1. Susanne trifft (Thomas)
   - a. er.
   - b. ihm.
   - c. ihn.

2. Lisa isst (eine Pizza)
   - a. sie.
   - b. ihr.
   - c. Sie.

3. Ich spreche mit (meinem Mann)
   - a. ihm.
   - b. er.
   - c. ihn.

4. David dankt (Susanne)
   - a. sie.
   - b. ihn.
   - c. ihr.

5. (Du und ich) freuen uns.
   - a. Sie
   - b. Ihr
   - c. Wir

6. (David) liest das Buch.
   - a. Ihn
   - b. Er
   - c. Ihm

4

Read the English sentences on the left and match them with the correct German translation. Try to memorize as they are very useful in everyday conversation.

1. *I am bored.*
2. *You hurry.*
3. *I thank you (informal).*
4. *I am sorry.*
5. *How are you?*
6. *What's the time?*
7. *We thank you (polite).*
8. *We are sorry.*
9. *You are looking forward to ...*
10. *Enjoy yourselves.*

a. Ihr freut euch auf ...
b. Wie geht es dir?
c. Wir danken Ihnen.
d. Wir entschuldigen uns.
e. Du beeilst dich.
f. Amüsiert euch gut.
g. Ich danke dir.
h. Es tut mir Leid.
i. Ich langweile mich.
j. Wie spät ist es?

1 TR. 62

Look at the pictures to see what people do not like to eat or drink. Try to match the pictures with the sentences below.

You may also listen to these sentences on the CD.

1 
______

2 
______

3 
______

4 
______

5 
______

a. David trinkt keinen Alkohol.

b. Melanie isst keine Schokolade.

c. Susanne mag keine Nudeln.

d. Lisa isst keinen Fisch.

e. Thomas trinkt kein Bier.

§ 11 Negation

Gut zu wissen

kein, **keine** and **keinen** negate the noun that follows. **Thomas trinkt kein Bier**. *Thomas doesn't drink beer.*

2 TR. 63

Read the questions on the left hand side match them to the answers on the right. These sentences are also included on the CD.

1. Gehen wir ins Kino?
2. Kommst du mit?
3. Lädst du Lisa ein?
4. Holst du Melanie ab?
5. Kommen Sie aus England?
6. Möchtest du einen Kaffee mit mir trinken?

a. Nein, wir kommen nicht aus England.
b. Nein, Lisa lade ich nicht ein.
c. Nein, ich komme nicht mit.
d. Nein, danke.
e. Nein, ich hole sie nicht ab.
f. Ich kann nicht ins Kino gehen, ich arbeite.

Gut zu wissen

Nein is the simple answer *no*.
nicht (*not*) negates a whole sentence or the word(s) that follow(s).

3 TR. 64

David and Melanie invite the Kowalskis for dinner. Read the dialogue paying special attention to how the sentences and single words are negated.

Thomas: Kowalski.
David: Hallo, Thomas. Hier ist David.
Thomas: Hallo David. Wie geht's dir?
David: Danke gut. Hör mal, habt ihr morgen Abend Zeit?
Thomas: Morgen Abend? Ja, warum?
David: Wir möchten euch zum Essen einladen.
Thomas: Das ist aber nett. Um wie viel Uhr?
David: So um sieben? Oder ist das zu spät?
Thomas: Nein, das ist nicht zu spät. Sollen wir etwas mitbringen?
David: Nein, nicht nötig. Melanie bereitet alles vor. Es gibt Fisch.
Thomas: Oh ...
David: Oder esst ihr keinen Fisch?
Thomas: Doch, doch ... ich mag sehr gerne Fisch und Susanne auch, aber Lisa nicht.
David: Warte einen Moment. Melanie, Lisa mag keinen Fisch.
Melanie: Gib mir bitte das Telefon. Hallo, Thomas. Kein Problem. Ich koche Nudeln für Lisa.
Thomas: Mach dir nicht so viel Arbeit, Melanie.
Melanie: Ach, was. Das ist doch keine Arbeit.
Thomas: Na dann, danke für die Einladung. Sollen wir etwas mitbringen?
Melanie: Nein, nein. Nur gute Laune und viel Hunger.
Thomas: Gut, dann bis morgen. Tschüss.
Melanie: Ich freue mich. Bis dann.
Thomas: Susanne, die Simmons haben uns morgen Abend zum Essen eingeladen.
Susanne: Klasse. Dann muss ich nicht kochen. Was gibt es?
Thomas: Es gibt Fisch.
Lisa: Ich komme nicht mit. Ich mag keinen Fisch.
Thomas: David hat dich auch nicht eingeladen ...
Susanne: Sie haben Lisa nicht eingeladen??
Thomas: Natürlich haben die Simmons Lisa eingeladen. Sie muss auch keinen Fisch essen. Melanie macht Nudeln für Lisa.
Susanne: Was bringen wir mit?
Thomas: Ich weiß nicht. Vielleicht eine Flasche Wein?
Suzanne: Nein, das ist keine gute Idee. Ich glaube, David trinkt keinen Alkohol.
Thomas: Schokolade? David liebt Schokolade.
Suzanne: Aber Melanie isst keine Schokolade. Weißt du was? Wir kaufen ihnen ein Buch über Katzen.
Thomas: Das ist gut. Beide mögen Katzen.

4 TR. 65

Kein is used to negate nouns with an indefinite or no article.

Das ist **eine** Katze.	Das ist **keine** Katze.
This is a cat.	lit.: *This is no cat.*

Kein is like a negative article: it appears directly before the noun that is negated and the ending changes according to the gender of the noun and the case.

	masculine	feminine	neuter
nom.	kein	kein**e**	kein
acc.	kein**en**	kein**e**	kein
dat.	kein**em**	kein**er**	kein**em**

Unlike the indefinite article, **kein** has a plural.

nom.	kein**e**
acc.	kein**e**
dat.	kein**en**

Ich habe Freunde.	Ich habe **keine** Freunde.
I have friends.	lit.: *I have no friends.*

▸ § 11 Negation

nicht + ~~ein~~ → kein

nicht + ~~eine~~ → keine

nicht + ~~einen~~ → keinen

5

Complete the sentences by writing the correct form of **kein** into the gap.

1. David trinkt ________________ Alkohol.
2. Die Simmons mögen ________________ Blumen.
3. Lisa mag ________________ Fisch.
4. Melanie isst ________________ Fleisch.
5. Wir haben ________________ Zeit.
6. Das ist ________________ gute Idee.
7. Er hat ________________ Freunde.
8. David will ________________ Buch über Katzen.

▸ § 11 Negation

Gut zu wissen

Nouns with a definite article are negated with **nicht**.
Ich mag die Katze nicht. *I don't like the cat.*
Nouns with an indefinite article or no article are negated with **kein.**
Ich mag keine Katzen. *I don't like cats.*

6 TR.66

The word **nicht** (*not*) negates a whole sentence or part of a sentence. When the whole sentence is negated, **nicht** is placed at the end of the sentence.

> Wir besuchen die Simmons **nicht.**
> *We don't visit the Simmons.*

When only a part of the sentence is negated, **nicht** is placed before the elements in question.

> David trifft **nicht** Susanne. Er trifft Thomas.
> *David doesn't meet Susanne. He meets Thomas.*

These examples are also included on the CD.

7

The following elements are positioned behind the negation **nicht:**

The infinitive that goes together with modal verbs:
> Susanne **muss nicht kochen.**
> Ich **kann nicht gut kochen.**

The prefix of separable verbs:
> Wir **laden** Lisa **nicht ein.**
> Ich komme **nicht mit.**

Adjectives (when used with **sein**):
> Die Idee ist **nicht gut.**
> Sieben Uhr ist **nicht zu spät.**

Prepositional phrase:
> Die Simmons kommen **nicht aus Köln.**
> David geht **nicht zur Party.**

The participle in the perfect tense:
> Thomas **hat** Melanie **nicht eingeladen.**

8

Negate the following sentences.

1. Wir kommen heute. ____________________
2. Thomas telefoniert mit Melanie. ____________________
3. Suzanne kocht morgen. ____________________
4. Ich mag die Katze von Melanie. ____________________

9

These sentences are mixed up. Put them into the correct order. Pay special attention to the position of the negation **nicht.**

1. David / nicht / kann / kochen / .

   ____

2. mit / kommt / Lisa / nicht / .

   ____

3. Ich / dich / hole / ab / nicht / .

   ____

4. ist / Sieben / Uhr / zu / nicht / spät / .

   ____

5. ist / Die Idee / gut / nicht / .

   ____

6. nicht / Das / mein / ist / Bier / .

   ____

7. Melanie / aus / kommt / nicht / England / .

   ____

10

Now you know which elements are always positioned behind the negation **nicht**. Try to translate the following sentences into German paying special attention to the position of **nicht**.

1. Susanne doesn't have to cook. ____________________
2. We don't invite Lisa. ____________________
3. The idea is not good. ____________________
4. The Simmons are not from Cologne. ____________________
5. I can't cook well. ____________________
6. Thomas didn't invite Melanie. ____________________
7. Seven o'clock is not too late. ____________________
8. I don't come along. ____________________
9. David doesn't go to the party. ____________________

11

You can answer a question by saying **ja** (*yes*) or **nein** (*no*).
In German there is a third possibility: **doch**. **Doch** is an affirmative answer to a negative question.

Isst du **keinen** Fisch?
Doch, ich mag Fisch.

Now read the questions. The brackets indicate if your answer is affirmative (+) or negative (-). Mark the correct answer.

1. Sind Sie Thomas Kowalski? (-)
   - a. Nein, ich bin nicht Thomsas Kowalski.
   - b. Ja, ich bin Thomas Kowalski.
   - c. Doch, ich bin Thomas Kowalski.

2. Isst Susanne keinen Fisch? (+)
   - a. Ja, sie isst Fisch.
   - b. Nein, sie isst keinen Fisch.
   - c. Doch, sie isst Fisch.

3. Mögen die Simmons Katzen? (+)
   - a. Ja, sie mögen Katzen.
   - b. Nein, mögen keine Katzen.
   - c. Doch, sie mögen Katzen.

4. Habt ihr keine Zeit? (-)
   - a. Doch, wir haben Zeit.
   - b. Ja, wir haben Zeit.
   - c. Nein, wir haben keine Zeit.

12

The negation **nicht** is valid for a specific situation.

David kommt (heute, morgen, ...) nicht mit ins Kino.
David doesn't come along to the movies. (not today, not tomorrow, but maybe next week...)
Thomas trinkt das Bier nicht aus.
Thomas doesn't finish the beer. (not this beer, but he usually finishes his drinks)

Nie (*never*) is valid for all times:
David kommt nie mit ins Kino.
David never comes along to the movies. (not today, not tomorrow, not last week, ...)
Melanie isst nie Fleisch.
Melanie never eats meat. (She is a vegetarian.)
Thomas kommt nie pünktlich.
Thomas is never on time. (He is always 5 minutes late.)

13

Complete the sentences by writing the correct negation into the gap.

nicht - kein - nicht - keine - nicht - keinen - nicht - nicht

1. Wir kommen heute ____________.
2. Thomas telefoniert ____________ mit Melanie.
3. Das ist ____________ Fisch.
4. Melanie hat ____________ Katze.
5. Susanne kocht morgen ____________.
6. Ich trinke ____________ Wein.
7. Ich trinke den Wein ____________ aus.
8. Ich mag die Katze von Melanie ____________.

Gut zu wissen

As a very general rule you can remember that: **nicht** negates verbs, **kein** negates nouns.

14

Read the affirmative sentences and negate them.

1. Ich esse Fisch. ______________________________
2. Thomas trinkt Bier. ______________________________
3. Melanie mag Schokolade. ______________________________
4. Ich bin Thomas Kowalski. ______________________________
5. Ich komme mit. ______________________________
6. Wir laden Lisa ein. ______________________________

15

Split the chains of letters so that the sentences are correct. After doing that read them again. Do you notice the difference in meaning between the sentences using **nie** and **nicht**?

1. MelanieisstnieFleisch.
2. DavidkommtnichtmitinsKino.
3. DavidkommtniemitinsKino.
4. ThomastrinktdasBiernichtaus.
5. ThomastrinktdasBiernieaus.
6. Thomaskommtniepünktlich.

16

Look at the pictures and write the correct form of **kein** and the noun into the gap.

1. Melanie isst ____________ Schokolade.
2. Lisa isst ____________ Fisch.
3. Susanne mag ____________ Nudeln.
4. Thomas trinkt ____________ Bier.

17 TR. 67

Let's sum up what you have learned about negations. Look at the examples and mark the correct answer. These examples are also included on the CD.

1. Das ist kein Fisch.
   Kein *negates verbs / sentences / nouns.*
2. keinen Fisch, keine Katze, kein Bier
   Kein *changes its endings like the definite article / the indefinite article / adjectives.*
3. Ich habe keine Freunde.
   The negative article **kein** *has a plural / no plural.*
4. Ich will nicht.
   Nicht *negates nouns / verbs.*
5. Ich komme nicht mit. Nicht ich komme mit, David kommt mit.
   Nicht *changes its form / spelling / position.*
6. Isst du keine Nudeln? Doch, ich esse Nudeln.
   Nein / Doch / Ja *is an affirmative answer to a negative question.*

affirmative and negative answers

1

Read the question and the symbol in brackets. Give an affirmative (+) or a negative (-) answer. Which of the given answers is the correct one? Mark the box in front of the correct answer.

1. Telefoniert David mit Susanne? (-)
   - ■ a. Nein, er telefoniert mit Thomas.
   - ■ b. Ja, er telefoniert mit Susanne.
   - ■ c. Doch, er telefoniert mit Susanne.

2. Kocht Melanie Fisch? (+)
   - ■ a. Nein, sie kocht keinen Fisch.
   - ■ b. Doch, sie kocht Fisch.
   - ■ c. Ja, sie kocht Fisch.

3. Bringst du Blumen mit? (+)
   - ■ a. Ja, ich bringe Blumen mit.
   - ■ b. Doch, ich bringe Blumen mit.
   - ■ c. Nein, ich bringe keine Blumen mit.

4. Laden die Simmons Lisa nicht ein? (+)
   - ■ a. Nein, sie laden Lisa nicht ein.
   - ■ b. Ja, sie laden Lisa ein.
   - ■ c. Doch, sie laden Lisa ein.

5. Bringt Thomas keinen Wein mit? (-)
   - ■ a. Doch, er bringt Wein mit.
   - ■ b. Nein, er bringt keinen Wein mit.
   - ■ c. Ja, er bringt keinen Wein mit.

6. Mögen die Simmons keine Katzen? (+)
   - ■ a. Nein, sie mögen keine Katzen.
   - ■ b. Doch, sie mögen Katzen.
   - ■ c. Ja, sie mögen Katzen.

negation - questions

2

Nicht or **kein**? Write the correct negation into the gap.

1. Das ist ____________ Lisa, das ist Susanne.
2. Das ist ____________ gute Idee.
3. Die Idee ist ____________ gut.
4. Thomas mag ____________ Fisch.
5. Wir kommen ____________ mit zur Party.
6. Ich weiß ____________.
7. David hat ____________ Zeit.

3 TR. 68

What was your question again? Read the answers below and mark the box in front of the corresponding question.

1. Nein, ich esse kein Fleisch.
   - a. Isst du Fleisch?
   - b. Magst du kein Fleisch?
   - c. Isst du Fisch?

2. Doch, ich komme mit.
   - a. Kommst du mit?
   - b. Kommst du nicht mit?
   - c. Willst du mitkommen?

3. Nein, nicht nötig.
   - a. Magst du Bier?
   - b. Sollen wir etwas mitbringen?
   - c. Isst du Fisch?

4. Ja, wir haben Zeit.
   - a. Kochst du gut?
   - b. Hast du keine Zeit?
   - c. Habt Ihr morgen Zeit?

5. Er trinkt nie Alkohol.
   - a. Trinkt David Bier?
   - b. Magst du Bier?
   - c. Trinken wir ein Bier?

6. Doch, mir geht es gut.
   - a. Hast du Zeit?
   - b. Geht es dir gut?
   - c. Geht es dir nicht gut?

1 TR. 69

In this module we deal with prepositions. Look at the picture and read the sentences describing it below.

You may also listen to these prepositions on the CD.

Melanie sitzt **am** Tisch.
David steht **hinter** Melanie.
Susanne sitzt **neben** Thomas.
Thomas sitzt **zwischen** Susanne und Melanie.
Ein Stadtplan liegt **auf** dem Tisch.
Sie suchen **nach** der Straße.
Eine Lampe hängt **über** dem Tisch.
Die Katze sitzt **unter** dem Stuhl.
Die Pflanze steht **vor** dem Fenster.

Can you guess the translation of the prepositions used in the sentences with the help of the picture? Write the translation into the gap.

1. auf ______________
2. unter ______________
3. am ______________
4. hinter ______________
5. in ______________
6. über ______________
7. vor ______________
8. neben ______________
9. zwischen ______________

All these words are prepositions. Prepositions can have several meanings and functions. In this case they give information about the position of people/things.

2 TR. 70

Simmons is sick and has to see the vet. Read the dialogue below and paying special attention to the prepositions. Take a good look at the articles/pronouns that follow and the case they are in.

You may also listen to this dialogue while reading.

Melanie: Hallo Thomas. Unsere Katze ist krank und muss zum Tierarzt. Wir wollen zu Dr. Colani in der Sängerstraße.
David: Leider wissen wir nicht, wo die Straße ist. Hast du einen Stadtplan von Düsseldorf?
Thomas: Armer Simmons. Kommt in die Küche. Ich glaube, unser Stadtplan liegt hier auf dem Regal. Susanne legt ihn immer auf das Regal.
Melanie: Wo sind Lisa und Susanne?
Thomas: Lisa ist bei der Oma und Susanne ist beim Frisör, aber sie kommt bestimmt gleich nach Hause. So, ich lege den Stadtplan auf den Tisch und wir suchen nach der Sängerstraße.
Susanne: Hallo?
Thomas: Wir sind in der Küche.
Alle 3: Hallo Susanne.
David: Kennst du die Sängerstraße?
Susanne: Hallo, ihr drei. Die Sängerstraße?
Melanie: Ja, Simmons ist seit dem Wochenende krank und wir wollen mit ihm zu Dr. Colani in der Sängerstraße.
Susanne: Ich weiß auch nicht, wo die Sängerstraße ist. Wisst ihr was? Wir rufen in der Praxis an und sprechen mit Dr. Colani. Habt ihr die Telefonnummer?
Melanie: Moment ... Ein Freund hat mir die Nummer von Dr. Colani aus dem Telefonbuch auf einen Zettel geschrieben. Hier, bitte ...
Thomas: Danke. Wisst ihr was? Ihr habt die Namen verwechselt. Der Tierarzt heißt Sänger und die Straße heißt Colanistraße. Und die Colanistraße ist hier um die Ecke.
David: Können wir zu Fuß gehen oder sollen wir mit dem Auto fahren?
Thomas: Geht zu Fuß! Es ist ganz einfach: Ihr geht unsere Straße entlang, durch den kleinen Park bis zum Bäcker. Dann geht ihr an der Ampel über die Straße. Der Tierarzt ist neben dem Supermarkt.
Melanie: Vielen Dank für eure Hilfe!
Thomas: Gerne. Und gute Besserung für Simmons.

3 TR. 71

Read the sentences on the left and match them to the translation on the right.
You can also listen to these sentences on the CD.

1. Wir gehen zum Tierarzt.
2. Kommt in die Küche.
3. Ich suche nach dem Stadtplan.
4. Der Stadtplan liegt auf dem Tisch.
5. Sie suchen die Straße im Stadtplan.
6. Susanne kommt nach Hause.
7. Wir sind in der Küche.
8. Thomas spricht mit Dr. Colani.
9. Die Praxis ist neben dem Supermarkt.
10. Danke für eure Hilfe.

a. The surgery is next to the supermarket.
b. We are in the kitchen.
c. I'm looking for the streetmap.
d. Susanne comes home.
e. Come into the kitchen.
f. Thomas talks to Dr Colani.
g. The map is lying on the table.
h. They are looking for the street in the map.
i. Thanks for your help.
j. We go to see the vet.

4 TR. 72

There are seven prepositions that demand the accusative: **bis**, **durch**, **entlang**, **für**, **gegen**, **ohne** and **um**. The article or pronoun that follows has to be in the accusative case.
Take a closer look at the examples below. You may also listen to them on the CD.

§ 21 Prepositions

Gut zu wissen
Note that the preposition **entlang** is placed behind the noun.

durch – *through*

Gehen Sie **durch** den Park!	*Go* ***through*** *the park.*

bis – *until / till*: temporal meaning:

Ich warte **bis** Lisa kommt.	*I wait* ***until*** *Lisa comes.*

entlang - *along*

Geh die Straße **entlang**!	*Go* ***along*** *the street.*

für – *for*

Die Blumen sind **für** dich.	*The flowers are* ***for*** *you.*

gegen – *against*

Ich bin **gegen** das Einkaufszentrum.	*I am* ***against*** *the shopping mall.*

ohne – *without*

Wir fahren nicht **ohne** dich.	*We don't go* ***without*** *you.*

um - *around*

Die Sängerstraße ist **um** die Ecke.	*Sänger Street is* ***around*** *the corner.*

▶ § 21 Preposition

mit – *with*
nach – *to*
seit – *since*
zu – *to*
bei – *at*
gegenüber – *opposite*
von – *of*
aus – *from/out of*

5 TR. 73

These 8 prepositions demand the dative: **aus**, **bei**, **gegenüber**, **mit**, **nach**, **seit**, **von** and **zu**.
Read the sentences below paying special attention to the article or pronoun that follows the preposition.

These examples are also included on the CD.

Thomas spricht **mit** dir.
Thomas talks to you.

Wir fahren **nach** Düsseldorf.
We go to Düsseldorf.

Die Katze ist **seit** einem Tag krank.
The cat has been ill since yesterday.
Wir wollen **zu** Dr. Colani.
We want to see Dr. Colani.

Ist Lisa **bei** der Oma?
Is Susanne at work?

Der Frisör ist **gegenüber** der Schule.
The hairdresser is opposite the school.

Das ist ein Stadtplan **von** Düsseldorf.
This is a map of Düsseldorf.

Sie hat die Nummer **aus** dem Telefonbuch.
She has the number out of the phone book.

6 TR. 74

Complete the sentences by choosing the correct word.
All prepositions govern the dative case.

You can also find these sentences on the CD.

1. Melanie kommt aus *dem* / - / *der* Australien.
2. Ist Lisa bei *der* / *die* / *dem* Oma?
3. Das Museum ist gegenüber *dem* / *der* / *das* Kino.
4. Sprichst du mit *ich* / *mir* / *mich*?
5. Wir trinken nach *das* / *der* / *dem* Essen einen Kaffee.
6. Simmons ist seit *einem* / *einer* / *ein* Tag krank.
7. Die Praxis von *der* / - / *dem* Dr. Colani ist um die Ecke.

Gut zu wissen

Remember that proper names (family names, most countries, cities, etc.) do not use an article.
Wir sprechen mit Dr. Colani. Er spricht mit dem Tierarzt Dr. Colani in Düsseldorf.
Street names are an exception and do use articles: **Dr. Colani in der Sängerstraße.**

7 TR. 75

§ 21 Prepositions

The prepositions **an**, **auf**, **hinter**, **in**, **neben**, **über**, **unter**, **vor**, **zwischen** can take both the accusative and the dative case.

The preposition takes the accusative when the verb that precedes the preposition is dynamic and indicates a direction/change of position. The preposition answers the question:

Wohin? – *Where to*?
Ich gehe **in die** Küche. *I go* ***into*** *the kitchen.*

They take the dative when the preceding verb expresses a state/position and the prepositions answers the question:

Wo? – *Where*?
Wir sind **in der** Küche. *We are* ***in*** *the kitchen.*

Read some more examples. You can also listen to them on the CD.

Where to? Accusative	*Where? Dative*
Er setzt sich zwischen **die** Frauen.	Er sitzt zwischen **den** zwei Frauen.
Simmons setzt sich unter **den** Stuhl.	Simmons sitzt unter **dem** Stuhl.
Sie gehen **ins** Restaurant.	Sie essen **im** Restaurant.

8

Now try to complete the sentences below by writing the correct article or pronoun into the gaps.

1. Der Stadtplan liegt auf ____________ Regal.
2. Thomas legt den Stadtplan auf ____________ Regal.
3. Thomas sitzt neben ____________. (du)
4. Thomas setzt sich neben ____________. (du)
5. Die Pflanze steht vor ____________ Fenster.
6. Wir stellen die Pflanze vor ____________ Fenster.

Gut zu wissen

The following prepositions are usually contracted with the definite article:
in + das = **ins**,
in + dem = **im**,
an + dem = **am**,
zu + dem = **zum**,
bei + dem = **beim**,
auf + das = **aufs**,
an + das = **ans**.

9

Some prepositions also have other meaning. Read the explanation below.

in also has a temporal meaning:

in zwei Tagen	*in two days*

In this meaning in takes the dative.

um is also used to express a time:

um 20 Uhr	*at 8 pm*

auf is often used with offices and official institutions:

aufs (**auf das**) **Rathhaus**	*to the townhall*

an can also have a temporal meaning and is used for example with week-days:

am Samstag	*on Saturday*

aus is also used to give information about material:

aus Baumwolle	*out of cotton*

bei is also used with companies:

Ich arbeite bei …	*I work for/at …*

10 TR. 76

1

2

3

4

5

Look at the pictures and write the correct preposition into the gaps.

You also find these sentences on the CD.

1. Der Film beginnt ____________ 20 Uhr.
2. Paul hat ____________ Samstag Geburtstag.
3. Mein T-Shirt ist ____________ Baumwolle.
4. Lisas Oma kommt ____________ 2 Tagen.
5. Ich arbeite ____________ Airlines International.

11

Verbs often govern specific prepositions. You know the following expressions from the dialogue and other exercises. Write the the correct preposition into the gaps. Look at the **Gut zu wissen** box for a clue.

1. Ich danke dir ____________ die Hilfe.
2. Wir freuen uns ____________ heute Abend.
3. Die Simmons laden die Kowalskis ____________ Essen ein.
4. Sie suchen ____________ der Sängerstraße.
5. Wir treffen uns heute ____________ Freunden.
6. Wir gratulieren Paul ____________ seinem 70. Geburtstag.
7. Susanne interessiert sich ____________ Kunst.
8. Melanie freut sich ____________ das Buch.

Gut zu wissen

Verbs with accusative:
danke für – *to thank for*
freuen auf – *to look forward to*
sich interessieren für – *to be interested in*
sich freuen über – *to be happy about something*
Verbs with dative:
einladen zu – *to invite for/to*
suchen nach – *to look for*
sich treffen mit – *to meet with*
gratulieren zu – *to congratulate on*

12

All of these prepositions take the accusative case. Complete the sentences with the correct article/pronoun. The word in brackets gives you a clue.

1. Ich warte bis ____________ kommt. (Lisa)
2. Gehen Sie durch ____________ Park! (der Park)
3. Gehen Sie ____________ Rhein entlang! (der Rhein)
4. David dankt Thomas für ____________ Hilfe. (sein)
5. Wir sind gegen ____________ neue Einkaufszentrum. (das Einkaufszentrum)
6. Ich gehe nicht ohne ____________ Thomas. (proper names)
7. Die Katze läuft um ____________ Stuhl. (der Stuhl)

13

Do you remember which prepositions take which case? Write the prepositions into two columns and try to memorize them.

durch den Park - aus dem Buch - gegen das Einkaufszentrum - die Straße entlang - von Düsseldorf - zu mir - für die Hilfe - ohne dich - um die Ecke - mit dir - beim Frisör - gegenüber der Schule

accusative	dative

14 TR. 11

Look at the picture and see where the person / thing is located. Then write the corresponding preposition into the gap.

1 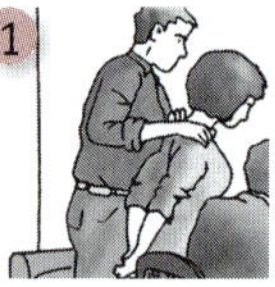
2 
3 
4 
5 

1. David steht ____________ Melanie.
2. Melanie sitzt ____________ Tisch.
3. Thomas sitzt ____________ Melanie und Susanne.
4. Die Lampe hängt ____________ dem Tisch.
5. Die Katze sitzt ____________ dem Stuhl.

15

Find the hidden German prepositions in the row of letters and mark them.

1. under	Übergegennebenunterdemauf
2. on	ansinnebenunteraufüber
3. into	nachvonzugegeninbis
4. next to	nebennachüberzwischen
5. (un)till	durchentlangbisohneum
6. through	gegenübermitseitvondurch

16

You know that dative / accusative prepositions take the accusative when the prepositions answer the question *where to*? and the verb indicates motion. Mark the sentences that answer the question *where to*?

1. ■ David steht **hinter seiner** Frau.
2. ■ David stellt sich **hinter seine** Frau.
3. ■ Simmons sitzt **unter dem** Stuhl.
4. ■ Simmons setzt sich **unter den** Stuhl.
5. ■ Sie gehen **ins** Restaurant.
6. ■ Sie essen **im** Restaurant.
7. ■ Thomas legt den Stadtplan **auf das** Regal.
8. ■ Düsseldorf liegt **am** Rhein.

Gut zu wissen

sich setzen (*to sit down*), (**sich**) **stellen** (*to place/put (oneself)*), **legen**, **gehen** indicate a change of place, motion and thus govern the accusative after the preposition. **sitzen** (*to sit*), **stehen** (*to stand*), **liegen** (*to lie*) are rather static and thus govern the dative after the preposition.

1

Match the pictures to the corresponding expressions.

1
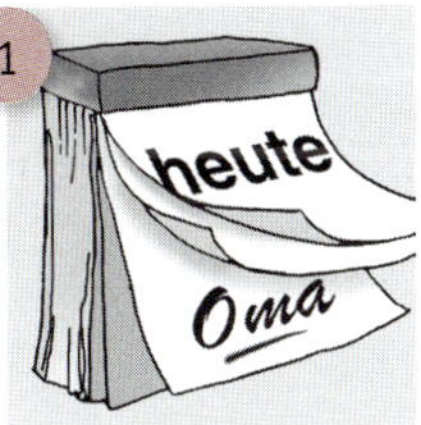

____

2
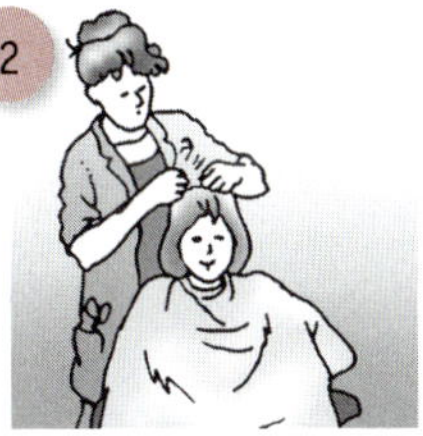

____

3

____

4

____

5

____

6

____

a. mit dem Auto fahren
b. neben dem Supermarkt
c. den Rhein entlang
d. in 2 Tagen
e. zu Fuß gehen
f. beim Frisör

2

Complete the sentences by choosing the correct preposition.

1. David stellt sich *hinter / gegen / bei* seine Frau.
2. Thomas setzt sich *nach / zu / an* den Tisch.
3. Ich warte *seit / bis / um* Lisa kommt.
4. Simmons ist *bis / seit / um* einem Tag krank.
5. Melanie freut sich *in / für / über* das Buch.
6. Susanne interessiert sich *nach / für / mit* Kunst.
7. David fährt *von / ohne / mit* dem Auto.

prepositions

3 TR. 78

What can you see in the pictures? Mark the correct sentence. All sentences are also included on the CD.

1

- a. Die Pflanze steht vor dem Fenster.
- b. Die Pflanze steht neben dem Fenster.
- c. Die Pflanze steht unter dem Fenster.

2

- a. Wir gehen in den Park spazieren.
- b. Wir gehen durch den Park.
- c. Wir gehen im Park spazieren.

3

- a. Lisas Oma kommt um 2 Uhr.
- b. Lisas Oma kommt für 2 Tage.
- c. Lisas Oma kommt in 2 Tagen.

4

- a. Ich arbeite bei Airlines International.
- b. Ich arbeite in Düsseldorf.
- c. Ich komme aus Australien.

5

- a. Der Film beginnt um 20 Uhr.
- b. Der Tierarzt ist um die Ecke.
- c. Geht die Straße entlang.

6

- a. Gehen Sie über die Straße.
- b. Gehen Sie den Fluss entlang.
- c. Gehen Sie durch den Park.

1 TR. 79

In this module we deal with interrogatives. Look at the invitation card and read the bits of information. Each bit gives an answer to a different w-word. How many w-words in German do you know? In the word box on the right you find some of them together with the English translation.

They are also included on the CD.

wer - *who*
was - *what*
wann - *when*
wie - *how*
wohin – *where to*
warum - *why*
wo - *where*

2

Read the questions on the left and the answers on the right. Match the answer to the corresponding question.

Gut zu wissen

Note that questions with interrogatives are answered with a complete sentence.

1. Wann hat Thomas Geburtstag?
2. Was wünschst du dir?
3. Wen hast du eingeladen?
4. Woher kommt Carl?
5. Wo ist der Picknickkorb?
6. Wer ist Dan?
7. Wie ist das Wetter am Sonntag?

a. Ich hoffe, dass das Wetter schön ist.
b. Carl kommt aus Österreich.
c. Ich wünsche mir eine CD.
d. Der Picknickkorb ist in der Küche.
e. Er hat am Sonntag Geburtstag.
f. Ich habe meine Freunde eingeladen.
g. Dan ist Melanies Bruder.

3

Interrogatives ask for specific information: for a person, a thing, a location etc. A question with an interrogative follows the normal word order, i.e.: the verb is in the second position.

Wo bist du?	*Where are you?*

An answer to a question with an interrogative gives the required information.

Ich bin in der Küche.	*I am in the kitchen.*

Wer? (*who*) asks for a person (nominative)

Wer ist das?	*Who is that?*
Das ist Thomas.	*This is Thomas.*

Wen? (*who*) asks for a person (accusative)

Wen lädst du ein?	*Who do you invite?*
Ich lade dich ein.	*I invite you.*

Wem? (*whom*) asks for a person (dative)

Wem gibst du die Einladung?	*To whom do you give the invitation?*
Ich gebe sie dir.	*I give it to you.*

Was? (*what)* asks for a thing or activity

Was machst du?	*What are you doing?*
Ich lese.	*I am reading.*

Wo? (*where*) asks for a location, position

Wo wohnst du?	*Where do you live?*
In der Colanistraße.	*In Colani Street.*

Woher? (*where from*) asks for origin / direction

Woher kommt Melanie?	*Where is Melanie from?*
Aus Australien.	*From Australia.*

Wohin? (*where to*) asks for destination / direction

Wohin fahren wir?	*Where are we going?*
An den Rhein.	*To the river Rhine.*

Wann? (*when*) asks for time

Wann hat Thomas Geburtstag?	*When is Tom's birthday?*
Am Sonntag.	*On Sunday.*

Warum? (*why*) asks for reason

Warum kommt sie nicht?	*Why doesn't she come?*
Weil sie arbeitet.	*Because she works.*

Wie? (*how*) asks for characteristics

Wie ist das Wetter?	*What's the weather like?*
Schön.	*Fine.*

You can listen to the interrogative pronouns on the CD. You find a pronunciation tip in the **Gut zu wissen** box on the left.

Gut zu wissen

The German **w** is like the English v (as in victory): Put your front teeth on your lower lip and breathe out making a humming sound.

4

Read the answers and complete the questions by writing the correct interrogative pronoun.

1. ____________	liest du?	Ich lese ein Buch.
2. ____________	ist das?	Das ist Carl.
3. ____________	ist das Wetter?	Das Wetter ist schön.
4. ____________	feiert ihr?	Weil Thomas Geburtstag hat.
5. ____________	wohnst du?	Ich wohne in der Colanistraße.
6. ____________	ist das Picknick?	Am Sonntag.
7. ____________	fahren wir?	Wir fahren an den Rhein.
8. ____________	kommt Carl?	Er kommt aus Australien.

5

Yes / No questions start with the conjugated verb which is followed by the subject.

The answer to an affirmative yes / no question is **ja** or **nein**.

A negative yes / no question is answered with **nein** or **doch**.

Try to put the words into the right position in order to get correct yes / no questions.

1. Zeit / Hast / am / du / Sonntag / ?

   ____

2. Carl / ein / Lädst / du / ?

   ____

3. Thomas / ein / Schenkst / Buch / du / ?

   ____

4. nicht / Picknick / Kommst / zum / du / ?

   ____

5. ich / mitbringen / Soll / etwas / ?

   ____

Gut zu wissen

If the verb of the sentence is in first position, the word order is called inverted word order. The inverted word order is used in yes / no questions and imperative sentences.

▸ § 25 Subordinate clauses

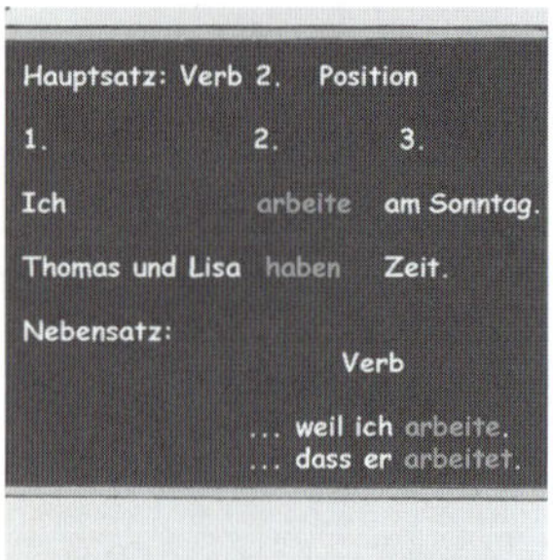

6

Compare the word order of the following sentences. Where is the verb positioned?

1. Ich **komme** nicht zum Picknick. — *I won't come to the pick-nick.*
2. Ich **arbeite** am Sonntag. — *I work on Sunday.*
3. Er **wünscht** sich eine CD. — *He wants a CD.*
4. Ich **komme** nicht, weil ich am Sonntag **arbeite.** — *I won't come because I have to work.*
5. Er **sagt**, dass er sich eine CD **wünscht.** — *He said he wants a CD.*

The first three sentences are main clauses.

Sentences four and five consist of a main clause (**Hauptsatz**) and a subordinate clause (**Nebensatz**) that complements the main clause.

In main clauses the conjugated verb is in the second position.
In subordinate clauses the conjugated verb is positioned at the very end.

The subordinate clause is introduced by a conjunction: (**Konjunktion**), here **weil** (*because*) or **dass** (*that*).

Main clause and subordinate clause are separated by a comma.

You can also find these sentences on the CD.

7

Read the sentences and decide if they are a simple main clause or a main clause with a subordinate clause. Mark the subordinate clauses.

1. ☐ Ich glaube nicht.
2. ☐ Er hat die CD von Elvis.
3. ☐ Ich glaube nicht, dass er die CD von Elvis hat.
4. ☐ Susanne hat nicht Geburtstag.
5. ☐ Wir bringen nichts mit.
6. ☐ Susanne hat gesagt, dass wir nichts mitbringen sollen.
7. ☐ Thomas hofft, dass Carl mitkommt.
8. ☐ Wir machen ein Picknick.

8 TR. 82

A sentence starting with **weil** (*because*) gives a reason (**Grund**) for something.

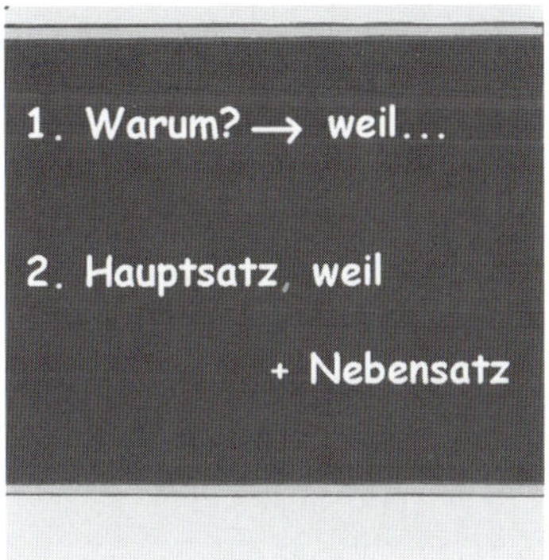

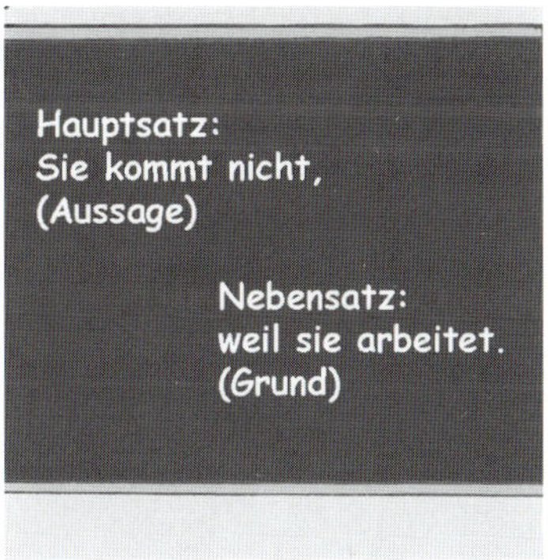

Warum kommt sie nicht? **Weil** sie arbeitet.

In this example the **weil**-sentence is the simple answer to the question **warum** (*why*).

Sie kommt nicht zur Party, **weil** sie arbeitet.

In the second example the weil-sentence is the explaining complement to the preceding assertion (**Aussage**). As such, **weil** is a conjunction between the main sentence and the subordinate clause.

The examples are also included on the CD.

9

Now try to translate the sentences below. Remember, in subordinate clauses the conjugated verb is positioned at the very end.

1. *Melanie speaks English because she comes from Australia.*

   ____

2. *We go to Dr Colani because the cat is sick.*

   ____

3. *I wear trousers because they are comfortable.*

   ____

10 TR. 83

The following sentences report a thought / wish, a speech, an opinion or a supposition. They consist of two parts: a main clause and a subordinate clause introduced by the conjunction **dass** (*that*).

Susanne sagt, **dass** Thomas sich eine CD wünscht. (reported speech)	*Susanne said that Thomas wants a CD for his birthday.*
Ich hoffe, **dass** das Wetter schön ist. (wish / expectation)	*I hope that the weather is nice.*
Ich denke, **dass** Susanne alles vorbereitet. (supposition)	*I think that Susanne prepares everything.*
Ich denke, **dass** ihm die Elvis CD gefällt. (opinion)	*I think that he likes the Elvis CD.*

You may listen to these sentences on the CD.

11 TR. 84

Gut zu wissen

Remember that in German subordinate clauses have two markers: they are introduced by a conjunction. The conjugated verb is always at the end.

Complete the sentences and put the words into the right position. You also find these sentences on the CD.

1. Thomas sagt, dass / wir / fahren / an den Rhein / .

____

2. Thomas sagt, dass / nichts / wir / müssen / mitbringen / .

____

3. Ich hoffe, dass / einen Kirschkuchen / backt / sie / .

____

4. Ich vermute, dass / auch / kommen / die Simmons / .

____

5. Ich glaube nicht, dass / kommt / Sylvia / .

____

12 TR. 85

Match the question on the left to the corresponding answer on the right.

You can also listen to them on the CD.

1. Warum trägst du keinen Rock?
2. Geht ihr ins Café?
3. Ist Dan Melanies Bruder?
4. Warum sprichst du Deutsch?
5. Kommt Carl?
6. Lädst du Corinna ein?

a. Ich hoffe, dass er kommt.
b. Weil ich Deutsch gelernt habe.
c. Nein, wir fahren an den Rhein.
d. Weil Hosen bequemer sind.
e. Nein, weil sie keine Zeit hat.
f. Ja, er ist Melanies Bruder.

13

Read the incomplete question and decide if it is a yes / no question or a question with interrogative. Write the correct interrogative into the gap.

Use the interrogative pronouns listed in the box below. Leave the gap empty for a yes / no question.

Wann – Was – Wo – Was - Wen

1. ______________ Kommst du zum Picknick?
2. ______________ hast du Geburtstag?
3. ______________ wünscht er sich?
4. ______________ ist das Picknick?
5. ______________ bringst du mit?
6. ______________ Sollen wir etwas mitbringen?
7. ______________ lädst du ein?
8. ______________ Lädst du Carl ein?

14

Read the following sentences and decide if the conjunction **dass** or **weil** is missing. Write the correct conjunction into the gap.

1. Wir machen ein Picknick, ________ Thomas Geburtstag hat.
2. Thomas hofft, ________ das Wetter schön ist.
3. Susanne sagt, ________ wir mit dem Fahrrad an den Rhein fahren.
4. Ich kaufe eine CD, ________ Thomas sich eine CD wünscht.
5. Wir bringen nichts mit, ________ Susanne alles vorbereitet.
6. Ich hoffe, ________ sie einen Kirschkuchen backt.
7. Carl kommt mit, ________ er am Sonntag nicht arbeiten muss.
8. Ich glaube nicht, ________ Sylvia Zeit hat.

15

What did he say? Convert the sentences below into a subordinate clause starting with:

Er sagte, dass ...

1. Ich komme nicht zum Picknick.

   ____

2. Das Wetter war schlecht.

   ____

3. Wir haben viel Spaß.

   ____

4. Ich fahre gerne Fahrrad.

   ____

5. Ich habe kein Auto.

   ____

6. Ich arbeite oft am Samstag.

   ____

7. Ich trage keine Röcke.

   ____

1

Which interrogative asks for what? Mark the correct box to answer the question.

1. **was** *asks for:*
   - *a. a person*
   - *b. a thing*
   - *c. the time*

2. **wer** *asks for:*
   - *a. a person*
   - *b. a thing*
   - *c. a characteristic*

3. **wie** *asks for:*
   - *a. the time*
   - *b. a characteristic*
   - *c. a place*

4. **warum** *asks for:*
   - *a. a movement*
   - *b. a person*
   - *c. a reason*

5. **wo** *asks for:*
   - *a. a movement*
   - *b. a place*
   - *c. a reason*

6. **wann** *asks for:*
   - *a. the time*
   - *b. a direction*
   - *c. a thing*

2

Complete the questions by choosing the correct word.

1. *Wann / Wer / Wie* hat Thomas Geburtstag?
2. *Mitbringt / Mitkommt / Kommt* Sylvia am Sonntag?
3. *Was / Warum / Wer* kommt Sylvia nicht?
4. *Wo / Woher / Was* kommt Carl?
5. *Wer / Was / Wem* wünscht sich Thomas?
6. *Hat / Glaubt / Denkt* er die CD von Elvis?
7. *Wem / Wer / Wen* lädst du ein?

subordinate clauses

3

Write the missing conjunctions (**dass** or **weil**) into the gaps.

1. Thomas lädt Freunde ein, ________ er Geburtstag hat.
2. Susanne glaubt, ________ das Wetter schön ist.
3. Susanne sagt, ________ wir mit dem Fahrrad an den Rhein fahren.
4. Ich kaufe eine CD, ________ Thomas sich eine CD wünscht.
5. Ich hoffe, ________ Susanne einen Kirschkuchen backt.
6. Carl kommt mit, ________ er am Sonntag nicht arbeiten muss.
7. Ich glaube nicht, ________ Sylvia Zeit hat.

4

Put the words into the right word order to form correct sentences.

1. Ich / mitkommst / dass / hoffe, / du / .

____

2. wir / fahren / Wann / an den Rhein / ?

____

3. kommt / Warum / Sylvia / nicht / ?

____

4. arbeiten / sie / Weil / muss / .

____

5. Thomas / Was / sich / wünscht / ?

____

6. er / glaube, / dass / Ich / möchte / eine CD / .

____

7. du / Wen / eingeladen / hast / ?

____

1

Module 1

Exercise 1
1g; 2i; 3c; 4h; 5f; 6e; 7a; 8d; 9b
Exercise 5
1 heißt; 2 wohnen; 3 kommt; 4 arbeite; 5 geht
Exercise 6
1.heiße; 2. wohnen; 3. kommen; 4. kenne;
5. arbeite; 6. geht; 7. können
Exercise 8
du nimmst; du liest; du fährst; er / sie / es nimmt; er / sie / es liest; er / sie / es fährt; ihr nehmt; ihr lest; ihr fahrt; sie / Sie nehmen; sie / Sie lesen; sie / Sie fahren
Exercise 9
1. sind; 2. ist; 3. bin; 4. sind
Exercise 11
1. Sie; 2. Sie; 3. Sie; 4. sie; 5. Sie
Exercise 12
1. a; 2. f; 3. d; 4. c; 5. b; 6. e
Exercise 13
1.geht; 2. lernt; 3. wohnt; 4. kommt; 5. heißt;
6. haben; 7. heißt
Exercise 14
1. Thomas fährt morgen nach Köln.
2. Susanne lernt morgen Englisch.
3. Nächstes Jahr fahren wir nach England.
4. Corinna Beck fährt nächstes Jahr nach Spanien.
5. Ihr habt in zwei Tagen Urlaub.
6. In zwei Tagen hast du Urlaub.

Exercise 16
short vowels
gibt; ist; nimmt
long vowels
liest; heißt; nehme; gehe; gebe

Test 1

Exercise 1
1. ihr; 2. ich; 3. wir; 4. er; 5. du; 6. Sie; 7. sie
Exercise 2
1. Sie; 2. Ich; 3. Sie / Wir; 4. Du; 5. Ihr
Exercise 3
1. d; 2. g; 3. b; 4. h; 5. a; 6. e; 7. f; 8. c
Exercise 4
1. Wie heißt du?
2. Ich bin David.
3. Wir wohnen in Düsseldorf.
4. Sind Sie Deutscher?
5. Ich komme aus England.
6. Sprechen Sie Deutsch?
7. Wir sprechen Deutsch und Englisch.

2

Module 2

Exercise 1
1. das Kind; 2. die Frau; 3. das Glas; 4. der Mann; 5. das Fenster; 6. die Tasse; 7. der Stuhl; 8. der Tisch; 9. die Flasche
Exercise 2
1. a; 2. c; 3. b; 4. d
Exercise 5
1. einen; einen; ein; 2. eine; 3. ein; 4. eine;
5. die; das
Exercise 6
1. d; 2. c; 3. b; 4. a
Exercise 8
1. einen; 2. den; 3. eine; 4. ein
Exercise 10
1. der; 2. der; 3. dem; 4. den; 5. dem; 6. dem
Exercise 11
1. die; 2. ein; 3. der; 4. der; 5. ein; 6. das;
7. ein; 8. die
Exercise 12
1. einen; 2. einen; 3. eine; 4. ein; 5. den; 6. den
Exercise 13
1. einen; 2. -; 3. den; 4. einen; 5. den; 6. eine
Exercise 14
1. die Tochter; 2. der Nachbar; 3. der Tisch;
4. der Stuhl; 5. das Fenster; 6. die Tasse; 7. das Glas; 8. die Flasche
Exercise 15
1. eine; 2. einen; 3. ein; 4. -; 5. -; 6. -; 7. Melanie Simmons
Exercise 16
1. die; 2. eine; 3. den; einen

Module 2 bis 3

Test 2
Exercise 1
1. -; 2. ein; 3. -; 4. -; 5. eine; 6. die
Exercise 2
1. die; 2. der; 3. das; 4. das; 5. der; 6. die; 7. die; 8. der; 9. der; 10. das
Exercise 3
1. dem; 2. dem; 3. der; 4. den; 5. einem; 6. den; 7. dem
Exercise 4
1. eine; 2. einen; 3. einen; 4. einen; 5. ein; 6. einen; 7. einen; 8. ein; 9. einen

3

Module 3
Exercise 1
1. das Büro; 2. der Stuhl; 3. der Computer; 4. das Telefon; 5. das Papier; 6. die Firma; 7. die Zeitung; 8. der Kuli
Exercise 2
1. f; 2. a; 3. e; 4. h; 5. j; 6. d; 7. i; 8. g; 9. c; 10. b
Exercise 4
1. die Bäckerin; 2. die Metzgerin; 3. der Verkäufer; 4. die Kellnerin; 5. der Lehrer; 6. der Apotheker; 7. der Kassierer
Exercise 6
DER: Stadtteil; Parkplatz; Stadtplan; Park; Bahnhof
DIE: Fußgängerzone; Straße; Stadt; Kirche; Polizei
DAS: Rathaus; Museum; Kino; Einkaufszentrum; Geschäft
Exercise 7
Singular: der Beruf; der Kollege; das Büro; der Computer; die Sekretärin; die Firma
Plural: die Berufe; die Kollegen; die Büros; die Computer; die Sekretärinnen; die Firmen
The plural definite article is always **die**.
Exercise 8
1. die Bäckerinnen; 2. die Sekretärinnen; 3. die Apothekerinnen; 4. die Lehrerinnen;
5. die Ärztinnen; 6. die Kassiererinnen; 7. die Kellnerinnen
Exercise 9
1. der Bäcker; 2. das Glas; 3. der Computer; 4. das Kino; 5. der Mann; 6. die Frau; 7. das Foto; 8. die Blume; 9. der Bahnhof; 10. der Park
Exercise 10
1. die Supermärkte; 2. die Apotheken; 3. die Straßen; 4. die Firmen; 5. die Kinder; 6. die Stühle; 7. die Kirchen; 8. die Nachbarn; 9. die Stadtpläne; 10 die Lehrer
Exercise 12
1. die Kinder; 2. den Kindern; 3. die Frauen; 4. den Frauen; 5. Die Männer; 6. den Männern
Exercise 13
1. Jungen; 2. Kindern; 3. Töchtern; 4. Nachbarn; 5. Computern; 6. Kindern; 7. Männern; 8. Frauen; 9. Kollegen
Exercise 15
1. die Kollegen; 2. einen Kollegen; 3. der Kollege; 4. dem Kollegen; 5. den Kollegen; 6. die Kollegen
Exercise 16
1. der Bürostuhl; 2. der Computertisch; 3. das Blumengeschäft; 4. die Haustür; 5. der Stadtteil; 6. der Straßenname
Exercise 17
1. die Lehrerin; 2. die Ärztin; 3. die Bäcker; 4. der Kellner; 5. die Verkäuferinnen

Test 3
Exercise 1
1. a; 2. a; 3. c; 4. b
Exercise 2
1. e; 2. d; 3. f; 4. b; 5. a; 6. c
Exercise 3
1. das Blumengeschäft; 2. der Bürostuhl; 3. der Computertisch; 4. der Stadtplan; 5. die Speisekarte; 6. die Kaffeetasse; 7. der Straßenname
Exercise 4
1. ein Junge; 2. einen Namen; 3. einen Beruf; 4. den Männern; 5. Töchter

4

Module 4

Exercise 1

1. g; 2. e; 3. j; 4. i; 5. h; 6. f; 7. a; 8. c; 9. d; 10. b

Exercise 5

1. an; 2. ab; 3. auf; 4. nach; 5. weg; 6. zu

Exercise 6

1. Susanne kauft im Supermarkt ein.
2. Sie gibt viel Geld aus.
3. David kommt nicht mit.
4. Bringst du Schokolade mit?
5. Melanie schlägt etwas anderes vor.
6. David räumt die Küche auf.

Exercise 7

inseparable verbs: bezahlen; genießen; empfehlen; erklären; vergessen

separable verbs: einkaufen; umrühren; ausruhen; mitbringen

Exercise 8

1. e; 2. i; 3. c; 4. a; 5. d; 6. h; 7. b; 8. j; 9. f; 10. g

Exercise 10

1. Trinken Sie viel Wasser.
2. Essen Sie mehr Fisch.
3. Hören sie mit dem Rauchen auf.
4. Kaufen Sie viel Gemüse.
5. Vergessen Sie Diäten.

Exercise 11

1. Iss Fisch!
2. Trink Milch!
3. Koch Kaffee!
4. Geh ins Kino!
5. Iss Gemüse!
6. Räume die Küche auf!

Exercise 12

1. Macht die Tür zu.
2. Bringt Schokolade mit.
3. Vergesst das Gemüse nicht.
4. Kauft die Bratwürstchen.
5. Räumt die Küche auf.
6. Wascht das Geschirr ab.

Exercise 14

Possible answers:

1. Trink bitte nicht so viel.
2. Bitte wasch das Geschirr ab.
3. Ruf doch mal Melanie an.
4. Komm doch bitte mit.
5. Denk doch bitte mal nach.
6. Ruh dich doch mehr aus.

Exercise 15

1. vergessen; 2. bezahlen; 3. einladen; 4. anrufen; 5. einkaufen; 6. ausruhen; 7. zumachen; 8. aufhören

a. vergessen; b. bezahlen

Exercise 16

Separable prefixes: zu-; nach-; an-; vor-; ein-; mit-; aus-

Inseparable prefixes: em-; ver-; be-; er-; ge-

Test 4

Exercise 1

1. a; 2. b; 3. b; 4. a; 5. b; 6. a

Exercise 2

1. anrufen; 2. abgeben; 3. weglassen; 4. umrühren; 5. mitkommen; 6. aufräumen

Exercise 3

1. m; 2. n; 3. f; 4. k; 5. j; 6. l; 7. d; 8. i; 9. e; 10. g; 11. a; 12. c; 13. b; 14. h

Exercise 4

1. kauft; 2. Bringst; 3. gibt; 4. Schlag; 5. rührt; 6. kommt

5

Module 5

Exercise 1

1. c; 2. e; 3. d; 4. b; 5. a; 6. f

Exercise 5

1. haben; 2. hat; 3. ist; 4. Sind

Exercise 6

1. b; 2. d; 3. e; 4. c; 5. a

Exercise 7

1. d; 2. e; 3. g; 4. f; 5. a; 6. b; 7. c

Exercise 9

1. b; 2. a; 3. c

Exercise 10
1. gekauft; 2. gereist; 3. gespielt; 4. gepackt; 5. geheiratet
Exercise 11
1. i; 2. e; 3. h; 4. f; 5. d; 6. a; 7. b; 8. g; 9. c
Exercise 13
1. verbracht; 2. gekannt; 3. gedacht; 4. mitgebracht
Exercise 14
1. Ich habe ein Flugticket gekauft.
2. Sie sind nach Mexiko gereist.
3. David hat Volleyball gespielt.
4. Italien hat uns gefallen.
5. Ich habe den Simmons den Schlüssel gegeben.
6. Ich habe Kataloge angesehen.
Exercise 15
1. gearbeitet; 2. gebucht; 3. gekauft; 4. geheiratet; 5. gemacht; 6. eingepackt; 7. ausgemacht; 8. eingekauft
Exercise 16
1. gegangen; 2. gesprochen; 3. gegessen; 4. getrunken; 5. geflogen; 6. angesehen; 7. mitgenommen; 8. weggefahren
Exercise 17
1. hat; 2. Seid; 3. sind; 4. hat; 5. bist; 6. sind; 7. habe
Exercise 18
1. gefallen; 2. geschrieben; 3. gekauft; 4. gemacht; 5. geschwommen; 6. getanzt; 7. gelegen

Test 5
Exercise 1
1. b; 2. a; 3. c; 4. b
Exercise 2
participle with ge-: buchen; ausmachen; wegfahren; spielen; arbeiten; geben
participle without ge-: verreisen; vergessen; empfehlen; fotografieren; gefallen; entschließen
Exercise 3
1. c; 2. b; 3. c; 4. a
Exercise 4
1. seid; 2. haben; 3. sind; 4. ist; 5. hast; 6. bin; 7. habe; 8. habt

6

Module 6
Exercise 1
1. f; 2. c; 3. e; 4. d; 5. a; 6. b
Exercise 3
1. h; 2. a; 3. i; 4. c; 5. d; 6. f; 7. e; 8. b; 9. g
Exercise 4
1. können; 2. können; 3. kannst
Exercise 6
1. kann; 2. können; 3. kannst; 4. Darf; 5. dürfen; 6. kann
Exercise 8
1. soll; 2. müssen; 3. müssen; 4. musst; 5. soll; 6. musst; 7. sollen
Exercise 9
1. a; 2. b; 3. b; 4. c; 5. a; 6. b
Exercise 11
1. Möchtest du einen Kaffee?
2. Ich möchte lieber einen Tee.
3. Melanie mag Vanilletee.
4. Ihr mögt Filme.
5. Möchtest du mit mir tanzen?
Exercise 13
1. muss; 2. darfst; 3. will; 4. sollt; 5. können; 6. mag; 7. könnt
Exercise 14
1. kann; 2. können; 3. darf; 4. kann; 5. darfst
Exercise 15
1. Ich mag Horrorfilme.
2. Ich kann Klavier spielen.
3. Ich muss viel arbeiten.
4. Ich mag Pizza.
5. Ich möchte einen Kaffee trinken.
6. Ich darf bis 22 Uhr lesen.
7. Ich soll mehr Gemüse essen.
8. Ich will Deutsch lernen.

Test 6
Exercise 1
1. a; 2. b; 3. b; 4. c; 5. b; 6. b
Exercise 2
1. Kannst du Klavier spielen.
2. Ich möchte ein Eis.

3. Susanne will eine Pizza essen.
4. Möchten Sie mit mir tanzen?
5. Ich will Deutsch lernen.
6. Soll ich dir helfen?

Exercise 3
1. muss; 2. soll; 3. sollst; 4. muss; 5. soll; 6. Soll; 7. soll; 8. müssen

Exercise 4
1. will; 2. muss; 3. will; 4. Möchten; 5. mögen; 6. darf; 7. sollst; 8. muss; 9. kann; 10. soll

7

Module 7

Exercise 1
1. d; 2. g; 3. e; 4. f; 5. b; 6. a; 7. c

Exercise 4
1. lebte; 2. wohnten; 3. arbeitete; 4. gratulierte

Exercise 5
ich atmete; du atmetest; er / sie / es atmete; wir atmeten; ihr atmetet; sie / Sie atmeten

Exercise 7
1. kam; 2. ging; 3. tranken; 4. hielten; 5. aß; 6. kam

Exercise 9
1. brachten; 2. wusste; 3. kannte; 4. rannten

Exercise 11
1. g; 2. d; 3. h; 4. c; 5. a; 6. i; 7. j; 8. b; 9. f; 10. e

Exercise 13
ich konnte, du konntest, er / sie / es konnte, ihr konntet, sie / Sie konnten
ich durfte, du durftest, wir durften, sie / Sie durften

Exercise 16
1. today; 2. first; 3. then; 4. always; 5. after; 6. earlier; 7. now; 8. never; 9. seldom

Exercise 17
1. Zuerst gratulierte der Bürgermeister.
2. Dann hielt Thomas eine Rede.
3. Danach sangen Birgit und Pierre ein Geburtstagslied.
4. Dann gab es Essen.
5. Und dann tanzten und feierten wir.
6. Ich war noch nie so glücklich.

Test 7

Exercise 1
1. b; 2. b; 3. a; 4. b; 5. c; 6. c

Exercise 2
ich musste, du musstest, er / sie / es musste, ihr musstet, sie / Sie mussten
ich sollte, du solltest, wir sollten, sie / Sie sollten

Exercise 3
1. waren; 2. konnten; 3. wurde; 4. aß; 5. gratulierte; 6. ging; 7. brachten mit; 8. rannten; 9. tanzten; 10. fotografierte; 11. spielte; 12. durfte

Exercise 4
Adverbs of frequency: oft; nie; selten; immer; manchmal
Adverbs of time: früher; heute; jetzt; nachher; morgen; dann

8

Module 8

Exercise 2
Definite article, accusative: den; die, das
Plural, accusative: die
Indefinite article, accusative: einen, eine, ein

Exercise 3
1. c; 2. e; 3. d; 4. a; 5. b

Exercise 4
1. Du bist schön.
2. Das Leben ist verrückt.
3. Die Kleidung ist teuer.
4. Röcke waren modern.
5. Paul ist alt.
6. Der Rock war kurz.

Exercise 7
schön, schöner, am schönsten
lang, länger, am längsten

Exercise 10
1. grüne; 2. rote; 3. helle; 4. kurzen; 5. bequeme

Exercise 11
1. die verrückten Schuhe; 2. den schönen Rock; 3. die praktische Hose; 4. den teueren Anzug; 5. das grüne Hemd

Exercise 13
1. normaler; 2. bequemen; 3. kurze; 4. schönes

Exercise 14
1. c; 2. b
Exercise 16
1. c; 2. f; 3. g; 4. i; 5. b; 6. h; 7. a; 8. e; 9. d
Exercise 17
1. roten, lange; 2. neu; 3. grünes; 4. groß;
5. kurzes, lange; 6. bequem
Exercise 18
1. Melanie ist größer als der Durchschnitt.
2. Der Rock ist so teuer wie das T-Shirt.
3. Eine Hose ist praktischer als ein Kleid.
4. Das Leben ist so verrückt wie eine Modenschau.
5. Lisa ist fast so groß wie Susanne.
6. Ein grünes Hemd ist schöner als ein roter Pullover.
7. Die lange Hose ist bequemer.

Test 8
Exercise 1
1. a; 2. a; 3. c
Exercise 2
Ich trage: 1. die langen Strümpfe; 2. den guten Pullover; 3. das kurze Kleid; 4. das große T-Shirt; 5. die rote Jacke
Exercise 3
groß, größer, am größten
praktisch, praktischer, am praktischsten
berühmt, berühmter, am berühmtesten
teuer, teurer, am teuersten
modern, moderner, am modernsten
gut, besser, am besten
kurz, kürzer, am kürzesten
alt, älter, am ältesten
Exercise 4
1. als; 2. wie; 3. als; 4. wie; 5. wie; 6. als;
7. wie; 8. als

9

Module 9
Exercise 1
1. d; 2. g; 3. f/h; 4. a; 5. h/f; 6. c; 7. b; 8. e
Exercise 3
1. meine; 2. deine; 3. unser
Exercise 5
1. f; 2. d; 3. e; 4. b; 5. g; 6. a; 7. h; 8. c
Exercise 8
1. seinem; 2. seiner; 3. ihrem; 4. ihren
Exercise 9
Ich sehe: seinen Vater; ihre Tochter; euer Kind; deine Mutter; eure Tochter; unseren Freund
Ich spreche mit: unserem Freund; eurem Nachbarn; deiner Mutter; seinem Vater; ihrer Tochter; eurer Tochter
Exercise 10
1. i; 2. e; 3. f; 4. h; 5. b; 6. d; 7. c; 8. j; 9. a;
10.g
Exercise 12
1. mich; 2. dich; 3. sich; 4. uns; 5. euch; 6. sich
Exercise 15
1. es; 2. euch; 3. sie; 4. ihn; 5. sie; 6. mich;
7. dich; 8. uns
Exercise 16
1. dir; 2. Ihnen; 3. mir; 4. uns; 5. ihm; 6. ihr;
7. euch; 8. ihnen
Exercise 19
Sentences 2, 3, 5, 6, 8 use reflexive verbs.
Exercise 20
1. mich; 2. sich; 3. uns; 4. sich; 5. euch; 6. sich;
7. dich

Test 9
Exercise 1
1. a; 2. c; 3. a; 4. b; 5. b; 6. c
Exercise 2
1. mich; 2. euch; 3. Ihr; 4. dich; 5. seine; 6. unsere; 7. euch
Exercise 3
1. c; 2. a; 3. a; 4. c; 5. c; 6. b
Exercise 4
1. i; 2. e; 3. g; 4. h; 5. b; 6. j; 7. c; 8. d; 9. a;
10. f

10

Module 10
Exercise 1
1. b; 2. d; 3. a; 4. c; 5. e

Exercise 2
1. f; 2. c; 3. b; 4. e; 5. a; 6. d
Exercise 5
1. keinen; 2. keine; 3. keinen; 4. kein; 5. keine; 6. keine; 7. keine; 8. kein
Exercise 8
1. Wir kommen heute nicht.
2. Thomas telefoniert nicht mit Melanie.
3. Susanne kocht morgen nicht.
4. Ich mag die Katze von Melanie nicht.
Exercise 9
1. David kann nicht kochen.
2. Lisa kommt nicht mit.
3. Ich hole dich nicht ab.
4. Sieben Uhr ist nicht zu spät.
5. Die Idee ist nicht gut.
6. Das ist nicht mein Bier.
7. Melanie kommt nicht aus England.
Exercise 10
1. Susanne muss nicht kochen.
2. Wir laden Lisa nicht ein.
3. Die Idee ist nicht gut.
4. Die Simmons kommen nicht aus Köln.
5. Ich kann nicht gut kochen.
6. Thomas hat Melanie nicht eingeladen.
7. Sieben Uhr ist nicht zu spät.
8. Ich komme nicht mit.
9. David geht nicht zur Party.
Exercise 11
1. a; 2. c; 3. a; 4. c
Exercise 13
1. nicht; 2. nicht; 3. kein; 4. keine; 5. nicht; 6. keinen; 7. nicht; 8. nicht
Exercise 14
1. Ich esse keinen Fisch.
2. Thomas trinkt kein Bier.
3. Melanie mag keine Schokolade.
4. Ich bin nicht Thomas Kowalski.
5. Ich komme nicht mit.
6. Wir laden Lisa nicht ein.
Exercise 15
1. Melanie isst nie Fleisch.
2. David kommt nicht mit ins Kino.
3. David kommt nie mit ins Kino.
4. Thomas trinkt das Bier nicht aus.
5. Thomas trinkt das Bier nie aus.
6. Thomas kommt nie pünktlich.
Exercise 16
1. keine; 2. keinen; 3. keine; 4. kein
Exercise 17
1. nouns; 2. the indefinite article; 3. has a plural; 4. verbs; 5. position; 6. doch

Test 10
Exercise 1
1. a; 2. c; 3. a; 4. c; 5. b; 6. b
Exercise 2
1. nicht; 2. keine; 3. nicht; 4. keinen; 5. nicht; 6. nicht; 7. keine
Exercise 3
1. a; 2. b; 3. b; 4. c; 5. a; 6. c

11

Module 11
Exercise 1
1. on; 2. under; 3. at; 4. behind; 5. in; 6. over; 7. in front of; 8. next to; 9. between
Exercise 3
1. j; 2. e; 3. c; 4. g; 5. h; 6. d; 7. b; 8. f; 9. a; 10. i
Exercise 6
1. -; 2. der; 3. dem; 4. mir; 5. dem; 6. einem; 7. -
Exercise 8
1. dem; 2. das; 3. dir; 4. dich; 5. dem; 6. das
Exercise 10
1. um; 2. am; 3. aus; 4. in; 5. bei
Exercise 11
1. für; 2. auf; 3. zum; 4. nach; 5. mit; 6. zu; 7. für; 8. über/auf
Exercise 12
1. sie; 2. den; 3. den; 4. seine; 5. das; 6. -; 7. den
Exercise 13
Accusative: durch den Park; die Straße entlang; für die Hilfe; gegen das Einkaufszentrum; ohne dich; um die Ecke

Dative: aus dem Buch; beim Frisör; gegenüber der Schule; mit dir; von Düsseldorf; zu mir
Exercise 14
1. hinter; 2. am; 3. zwischen; 4. über; 5. unter
Exercise 15
1. unter; 2. auf; 3. in; 4. neben; 5. bis; 6. durch
Exercise 16
2, 4, 5, 7
Test 11
Exercise 1
1. d; 2. f; 3. b; 4. e; 5. a; 6. c
Exercise 2
1. hinter; 2. an; 3. bis; 4. seit; 5. über; 6. für; 7. mit
Exercise 3
1. a; 2. b; 3. c; 4. a; 5. b; 6. b

12

Module 12
Exercise 2
1. e; 2. c; 3. f: 4. b; 5. d; 6. g; 7. a
Exercise 4
1. was; 2. wer; 3. wie; 4. warum; 5. wo; 6. wann; 7. wohin; 8. woher
Exercise 5
1. Hast du am Sonntag Zeit?
2. Lädst du Carl ein?
3. Schenkst du Thomas ein Buch?
4. Kommst du nicht zum Picknick?
5. Soll ich etwas mitbringen?

Exercise 7
3; 6; 7
Exercise 9
1. Melanie spricht Englisch, weil sie aus Australien kommt.
2. Wir gehen zu Dr. Colani, weil die Katze krank ist.
3. Ich trage Hosen, weil sie bequem sind.

Exercise 11
1. Thomas sagt, dass wir an den Rhein fahren.
2. Thomas sagt, dass wir nichts mitbringen müssen.
3. Ich hoffe, dass sie einen Kirschkuchen backt.
4. Ich vermute, dass die Simmons auch kommen.
5. Ich glaube nicht, dass Sylvia kommt.

Exercise 12
1. d; 2. c; 3. f; 4. b; 5. a; 6. e
Exercise 13
1. -; 2. Wann; 3. Was; 4. Wo; 5. Was; 6. -; 7. Wen; 8. -
Exercise 14
1. weil; 2. dass; 3. dass; 4. weil; 5. weil; 6. dass; 7. weil; 8. dass
Exercise 15
1. er nicht zum Picknick kommt.
2. das Wetter schlecht war.
3. wir viel Spaß haben.
4. er gerne Fahrrad fährt.
5. er kein Auto hat.
6. er oft am Samstag arbeitet.
7. er keine Röcke trägt.

Test 12
Exercise 1
1. b; 2. a; 3. b; 4. c; 5. b; 6. a
Exercise 2
1. Wann; 2. Kommt; 3. Warum; 4. Woher; 5. Was; 6. Hat; 7. Wen
Exercise 3
1. weil; 2. dass; 3. dass; 4. weil; 5. dass; 6. weil; 7. dass
Exercise 4
1. Ich hoffe, dass du mitkommst.
2. Wann fahren wir an den Rhein?
3. Warum kommt Sylvia nicht?
4. Weil sie arbeiten muss.
5. Was wünscht sich Thomas?
6. Ich glaube, dass er eine CD möchte.
7. Wen hast du eingeladen?

German Grammar overview

1. Adjectives
2. Adverbs
3. Article – definite
4. Article – indefinite
5. Comparison
6. Demostrative pronouns
7. Imperative
8. Interrogative pronouns
9. Masculine nouns in *–e*
10. Modal verbs
11. Negation
12. Nouns – gender
13. Nouns – singular
14. Nouns – plural
15. Word order
16. Past participle
17. Past tense
18. Perfect tense
19. Personal pronouns
20. Possessive pronouns
21. Prepositions
22. Present tense
23. Reflexive verbs
24. Separable verbs
25. Subordinate clauses
26. Verbs with prepositions

§ 1 Adjectives

1. Adjectives don't have an ending when they are used with the verb **sein** *(to be)*.
   Die Tür ist **grün**. – *The door is green.*
   Die Häuser sind **alt**. – *The houses are old.*
2. Adjectives have an ending when they describe or modify a noun.
   Die **grüne** Tür ist schön.
   The green door is nice.
   Die **alten** Häuser in Bonn.
   The old houses in Bonn.

Declination

The ending of the adjective depends on the case and the gender of the noun and whether you use the definite article **der** or the indefinite article **ein**.

Definite article + adjective (nominative case)

Singular

Masculine	*Feminine*	*Neuter*
der alt**e** Turm	die alt**e** Tür	das alt**e** Haus

Plural – *all gender*: die alt**en** Tische

Indefinite article + adjective (nominative case)

Singular

Masculine	*Feminine*	*Neuter*
ein alt**er** Turm	eine alt**e** Tür	ein alt**es** Haus

Plural – *all gender*: alt**e** Tische

Note: The adjectives **teuer** and **dunkel** drop the **e** when they are declined:
der **teure** Tisch – *the expensive table*
ein **dunkler** Turm – *a dark tower*

§ 2 Adverbs

Characteristics

The main characteristic of an adverb (= word that modifies the meaning of the verb) is that it isn't declined.

Adverbs of place:
hier *(here)*, **dort** *(there)*, **oben** *(up, upstairs, at/on the top)*, **unten** *(down, downstairs, at the bottom)*, **rechts** *(right)*, **links** *(left)*

Adverbs of time:
heute *(today)*, **morgen** *(tomorrow)*, **gestern** *(yesterday)*, **jetzt** *(now)*

Adverbs of frequency:
immer *(always)*, **nie** *(never)*, **zweimal** *(twice)*, **montags** *(every Monday)*

Adverbs of modality:
gern *(like to)*, **auch** *(also)*, **nur** *(only, just)*

Except for **gern**, none of the adverbs above can be compared.
Ich trinke **gern** Bier, mein Freund trinkt **lieber** Wein. Er mag **am liebsten** Rotwein.
I like drinking beer, my boyfriend prefers drinking wine. He likes red wine best of all.

Many adjectives can be used as adverbs. The forms are identical, also in the comparative and superlative:
Sabine kocht sehr **gut**.
Sabine cooks very well.
Sprich bitte **langsamer**!
Please speak more slowly!

Word order

In general, the adverb is placed behind the verb and in front of other elements like (a) prepositional phrases, (b) the word **nicht** or (c) an infinitive:

(a) Wir gehen **oft** ins Kino.
We often go to the cinema.
(b) Ich komme **morgen** nicht.
I don't come tomorrow.
(c) Du musst **rechts** abbiegen.
You have to turn right.

Adverbs of time often come first. The verb always remains in the 2nd position followed by the subject:

Morgen arbeite ich nicht.
I'm not working tommorrow.
Gestern war ich in Bonn.
I was in Bonn yesterday.

§ 3 Article – definite

In German, there are three articles for *the*: **der**, **die** and **das**. The article indicates the gender, the case and the number of the noun.

Declination

Singular	*Masculine*	*Feminine*	*Neuter*
Nom.	**der** Hund	**die** Katze	**das** Pferd
Acc.	**den** Hund	**die** Katze	**das** Pferd
Dat.	**dem** Hund	**der** Katze	**dem** Pferd

Plural	*All Gender*
Nom.	**die** Tiere
Acc.	**die** Tiere
Dat.	**den** Tieren

Use

You use the definite article when it is clear from the context which thing or person you mean:

Der Garten liegt hinter **dem** Haus.
The garden is behind the house.
Ich muss **den** Chef fragen.
I have to ask the boss.

The definite article is also used when you are thinking of one particular thing or person:

Hast du **die** Zeitung gesehen?
Did you see the newspaper?
Ich kenne **den** Freund von Maria nicht.
I don't know the boyfriend of Maria.

Without article

You don't use an article in the following cases:

1. Proper names:
Das ist **Herr Kowalski.** Seine Tochter heißt **Lisa.**
This is Mr. Kowalski. His daughter's name is Lisa.

2. Countries and towns:
Deutschland ist schön, oder?
Germany is beautiful, isn't it?
Wie gefällt dir **München**?
How do you like Munich?

But: Some countries are always used with the definite article: **die Schweiz** *(Switzerland)*, **die Türkei** *(Turkey)*.

3. Nationalities:
Sylvia ist **Österreicherin.** – *Sylvia is Austrian.*
Ich bin **Italiener.** – *I'm Italian.*

4. Job titles:
Er arbeitet als **Arzt.**
He works as a doctor.
Meine Mutter ist **Lehrerin.**
My mother is a teacher.

5. Uncountable nouns:
Ich kaufe **Reis**, **Milch** und **Zucker**.
I'm buying rice, milk and sugar.

6. Expressions with **haben**, **spielen**, **hören** and **machen:**
Ich habe Zeit. – *I have time.*
Er spielt Gitarre. – *He plays the guitar.*
Sie hört gern Musik.– *She likes listening to music.*
Das macht Spaß. – *That's fun.*

§ 4 Article – indefinite

The forms of the indefinite article depend on the gender, the case and the number of the corresponding noun.

Declination

Singular	*Masculine*	*Feminine*	*Neuter*
Nom.	**ein** Hund	**eine** Katze	**ein** Pferd
Acc.	**einen** Hund	**eine** Katze	**ein** Pferd
Dat.	**einem** Hund	**einer** Katze	**einem** Pferd

Note: The indefinite article has no plural forms.

Use

You use the indefinite article when it's the first time you talk about something or someone and when the noun is countable:

Hast du **ein** Haustier?
Do you have a pet?
Ich möchte **eine** Tasse Tee.
I'd like a cup of tea.

Compare also the use of the articles when the noun appears for the first and for the second time:

Ich lese **ein** Buch. **Das** Buch ist sehr interessant.
I'm reading a book. The book is very interesting.

There are two other grammar references that contain interesting information about the indefinite articles:
§ Negation informs you about the negated indefinite article **kein**.
§ Article – definite informs you about cases where you don't use an article at all.

§ 5 Comparison

Regular forms

Basic form	*Comparative*	*Superlative*
klein *(small)*	klein**er**	**am** klein**sten**
laut *(loud)*	laut**er**	**am** laut**esten**
alt *(old)*	**ä**lt**er**	**am ä**lt**esten**
dunkel *(dark)*	dunk**ler (!)**	**am** dunkelsten
teuer *(expensive)*	teu**rer (!)**	**am** teuersten

The comparative is formed by adding the ending **-er**.
The superlative ends in **-sten**. The ending **-esten** is used for adjectives in **-d**, **-t**, **-s**, **-ß**, **-sch** and **-z**.

Irregular forms

Basic form	*Comparative*	*Superlative*
groß *(big)*	größer	am grö**ß**ten
hoch *(high)*	hö**h**er	am hö**ch**sten
nah *(near)*	näher	am nä**ch**sten
gut *(good)*	**besser**	am **besten**
viel *(much)*	**mehr**	am **meisten**

Umlauts in the comparative and superlative

Especially one-syllable adjectives often take an umlaut:

a ▸ ä: alt *(old)* ▸ **ä**lter, am **ä**ltesten
Also: hart *(hard)*, lang *(long)*, nah *(near)*, kalt *(cold)*, warm *(warm, hot)*
o ▸ ö: groß *(big)* ▸ gr**ö**ßer, am gr**ö**ßten
Also: hoch *(high)*
u ▸ ü: jung *(young)* ▸ j**ü**nger, am j**ü**ngsten
Also: kurz *(short)*, gesund *(healthy)*

Use

1. Expressing that two items or qualities are similar:
   so / genauso + basic form + **wie**
   Bananen sind **so** teuer **wie** Äpfel.
   Bananas are as expensive as apples.
   Maria ist **genauso** alt **wie** du.
   Maria is just as old as you are.

▼

2. Comparing one person, thing or quality to another:
   comparative + **als**
   Ich bin **älter als** meine Schwester.
   I'm older than my sister.
   Im Garten ist es **schöner als** auf dem Balkon.
   In the garden it's nicer than on the balcony.

§ 6 Demonstrative pronouns

Dieser, diese, dieses

The demonstrative pronoun **dieser** *(this)* has the same endings as the definite article.

Singular	*Masculine*	*Feminine*	*Neuter*
Nom.	dies**er** Mann	dies**e** Frau	dies**es** Kind
Acc.	dies**en** Mann	dies**e** Frau	dies**es** Kind
Dat.	dies**em** Mann	dies**er** Frau	dies**em** Kind

Plural	*All Gender*
Nom.	dies**e** Personen
Acc.	dies**e** Personen
Dative	dies**en** Personen

Use

The demonstrative pronoun **dieser** is used if you want to point to something or someone close to you:
Was kostet **diese** Tasche?
How much does this bag cost?

It is used when you want to point to something or someone mentioned shortly before:
Neanderstraße ...? Ich kenne **diese** Straße nicht.
Neander Street ...? I don't know this street.

Der, die, das emphasized

	Singular		Plural	
	Masc.	*Fem.*	*Neuter*	*All Gender*
Nom.	**der**	**die**	**das**	**die**
Acc.	**den**	**die**	**das**	**die**
Dat.	**dem**	**der**	**dem**	**denen**

The forms of the demonstrative pronoun and the definite article are identical apart from the dative plural.
Article: **den** – demonstrative pronoun: **denen.**

Use

The demonstrative pronoun refers to a noun mentioned before and it is used to avoid the repetition of the noun.
Wo ist der Papagei? – **Der** ist in seinem Käfig.
Where is the parrot? – It is in its cage.
Gefällt dir der Schrank? – **Den** finde ich hässlich.
Do you like the cupboard? – I find it ugly.

Special use of **das**: to refer to the complete information given before you use the pronoun **das**.
Er ist nicht gekommen. **Das** verstehe ich nicht.
He didn't come. I don't understand that.
Du bist schüchtern. **Das** glauben wir nicht.
You are shy. We don't believe that.

Note that the demonstrative pronoun is placed in front of the verb and it is emphasized.

§ 7 Imperative

The imperative forms are quite regular, apart from the verb **sein.**

Conjugation

	gehen	nehmen	sein
du:	geh!	nimm!	sei!
ihr:	geht!	nehmt!	seid!
Sie:	gehen Sie!	nehmen Sie!	seien Sie!

The regular forms of the imperative are derived from the present tense.

Du-form: You have to drop the ending **-st** and the personal pronoun.

Ihr-form: You just have to drop the personal pronoun.

Sie-form: This form is just inverted.

Verbs ending in **-gen**, **-den** or **-ten** form the 2nd person singular (**du**-form) by adding an **-e**:

entschuldigen ▸ entschuldig**e**! – *Excuse me!*
reden ▸ red**e**! – *Speak!*
warten ▸ wart**e**! – *Wait a moment!*

Verbs with irregularities in the **du**-form:

fahren ▸ **fahr**! – *go!*
lesen ▸ **lies**! – *read!*
haben ▸ **hab**! – *have!*

Use

The imperative is used to give commands or make requests.

Geh nach Hause! – *Go home!*
Kommt mit! – *Come along!*
Seien Sie pünktlich! – *Be punctual!*

The imperative sounds less harsh when you add words like **bitte**, **doch** or **mal**.

Sei bitte pünktlich! – *Please be punctual!*
Geht doch nicht weg! – *Please don't go away!*
Geben Sie mir mal das Buch! – *Give me the book!*

Watch out for the word order: The imperative is the first word in the sentence!

§ 8 Interrogative pronouns

Here is a list of the interrogative pronouns from our course:

Wer ist dieser Mann?	*Who is this man?*
Was machst du heute?	*What are you doing today?*
Wen besuchst du?	*Who are you visiting?*
Wem gehört das?	*To whom does it belong?*
Wo wohnen Sie?	*Where do you live?*
Wohin gehst du?	*Where are you going?*
Woher kommst du?	*Where do you come from?*
Wann treffen wir uns?	*When do we meet?*
Wie geht es dir?	*How are you?*
Warum gehst du schon?	*Why are you going already?*

Another interrogative pronoun is **welcher** *(which)*. The endings of **welcher** are the same as of the definite article.

Welches Haus gefällt dir?
Which house do you like?
Welche Sprachen sprechen Sie?
Which languages do you speak?

Word order: In sentences with an interrogative pronoun, the verb is in the second position followed by the subject and the complements:

Wann kommst du nach Hause?
When are you coming home?

§ 9 Masculine nouns in *-e*

Masculine nouns ending in **-e** follow another declination pattern than all other nouns.
Masculine nouns in **-e** are:

der Deutsche *(German)*, der Pole *(Pole)*, der Russe *(Russian)*, der Türke *(Turkish)*, der Kollege *(colleague)*, der Neffe *(nephew)*, der Name *(name)*

Only the nominative singular ends in **-e.** All other cases, singular and plural, take the ending **-n.**

Nearly the same declination is also valid for der **Herr** *(sir, mister)* and **der Nachbar** *(neighbour)*.

Singular			
Nom.	der Türke	der Herr	der Nachbar
Acc.	den Türke**n**	den Herr**n**	den Nachbar**n**
Dat.	dem Türke**n**	dem Herr**n**	dem Nachbar**n**

Plural			
Nom.	die Türke**n**	die Herr**en**	die Nachbar**n**
Acc.	die Türke**n**	die Herr**en**	die Nachbar**n**
Dat.	den Türke**n**	den Herr**en**	den Nachbar**n**

▾

Some examples:
Meine Kollege**n** Mehmet und Dilek sind Türke**n**.
My colleagues Mehmet and Dilek are Turkish.
Wie sind deine Nachbar**n**? Sind sie nett?
How are your neighbours? Are they nice?
Ich muss Herr**n** Schmidt anrufen.
I have to call Mr. Schmidt.

Pay attention to the following important exception. In the nominative singular and plural you say:

	der Deutsche	die Deutsch**en**
but:	**ein** Deutsch**er**	Deutsch**e**

§ 10 Modal verbs

In German, there are six modal auxiliaries:

können	*to be able to, can*
wollen	*to want to*
müssen	*to have to, must*
dürfen	*to be allowed to, may*
sollen	*should, shall, to be supposed to*
mögen	*to like*

Conjugation

	können	wollen	müssen
ich	kann	will	muss
du	kannst	willst	musst
er/sie/es	kann	will	muss
wir	können	wollen	müssen
ihr	könnt	wollt	müsst
sie	können	wollen	müssen
Polite form:			
Sie	können	wollen	müssen

	dürfen	sollen	mögen
ich	darf	soll	mag
du	darfst	sollst	magst
er/sie/es	darf	soll	mag
wir	dürfen	sollen	mögen
ihr	dürft	sollt	mögt
sie	dürfen	sollen	mögen
Polite form:			
Sie	dürfen	sollen	mögen

The modal verbs are conjugated and they are usually followed by another verb in the infinitive form.

Ich will ausgehen. – *I want to go out.*

Use and word order

1. The modal is in the usual verb position: It comes second in assertions and in questions with interrogatives. In yes/no-questions it comes first.
   The infinitive form of the second verb is always at the very end of the sentence.
   Er **kann** nicht **schwimmen.**
   He cannot swim.
   Wir **wollen** nach Bonn **fahren.**
   We want to go to Bonn.
   Musst du heute **arbeiten**?
   Do you have to work today?
   Hier **darf** man nicht **weitergehen.**
   Here it's not allowed to go on.
   Wo **sollen** wir es **suchen**?
   Where should we look for it?
   Ich **mag** nicht Fußball **spielen.**
   I don't like playing soccer.
2. The infinitive can be dropped when it is already mentioned before.
   Willst du **mitkommen**? – Nein, ich **will** nicht.
   Do you want to come along? – No, I don't want to.
3. The modals **können**, **wollen** and **mögen** can also be used as full verbs without an infinitive.
   Er **kann** Französisch. *He can speak French.*
   Ich **will** einen Kaffee. *I would like a coffee.*
   Sie **mag** Kuchen. *She likes cake.*
4. If you want to have something, it's more polite to use the subjunctive form of **mögen**.
   Ich **möchte** ein Bier. – *I'd like a beer.*
   Ich **möchte** ein Bier **trinken.**
   I'd like to drink a beer.

The forms are regular:

Singular:	ich möchte, du möchtest, er/sie/es möchte
Plural:	wir möchten, ihr möchtet, sie möchten
Polite form:	Sie möchten

§ 11 Negation

Nein and doch

To answer a negated question you can use **nein** *(no)* or **doch** *(yes, I do)*. Compare:

Kommen Sie **nicht** mit?
– **Nein**, ich habe keine Zeit. *(negative answer)*
– **Doch**, ich komme mit. *(positive answer)*
Aren't you coming along?
– No, I don't have time.
– Yes, I'm coming.

Negation with nicht

To negate a sentence or a part of it you add **nicht** *(not)*. The position of **nicht** depends on whether you negate (a) only a word of the sentence or (b) the whole sentence. Compare:

(a) Ich besuche **nicht** meine Tante.
I'm not visiting my aunt (but another person).
(b) Ich besuche meine Tante **nicht**.
I don't visit my aunt.

If you want to negate the whole sentence, you have to place **nicht** at the end of the sentence.

But there are exceptions:

- **sein** + adjective:
  Das ist **nicht** möglich! – *That isn't possible!*
- **sein** + noun:
  Das ist **nicht** meine Tasche.
  That isn't my bag.
- Separable verb:
  Ich komme **nicht** mit. – *I don't come along.*
- Modal verb + infinitive:
  Ich kann **nicht** kommen. – *I can't come.*
- Perfect tense:
  Er hat **nicht** geschlafen. – *He didn't sleep.*
- Prepositional phrase:
  Ich fahre **nicht** nach Köln.
  I'm not going to Cologne.

Negation with kein

Kein is used to negate (a) a noun with an indefinite article and (b) a noun without an article.

Compare:

(a) Ich habe ein Auto. – *I've got a car.*
Ich habe **kein** Auto. – *I haven't got a car.*
(b) Sie ist Lehrerin. – *She's a teacher.*
Sie ist **keine** Lehrerin. – *She isn't a teacher.*

Declination

Singular	*Masculine*	*Feminine*
Nom.	kein Hund	kein**e** Katze
Acc.	kein**en** Hund	kein**e** Katze
Dat.	kein**em** Hund	kein**er** Katze

Singular	*Neuter*	*Plural All Gender*
Nom.	kein Pferd	kein**e** Tiere
Acc.	kein Pferd	kein**e** Tiere
Dat.	kein**em** Pferd	kein**en** Tieren

In the singular, **kein** is declined like the indefinite article **ein**. Unlike the indefinite article there are plural forms of **kein**.

Ich habe **keine** Haustiere.
I don't have got any pets.
Zwei Schiffe? Ich sehe **keine** Schiffe.
Two ships? I don't see any ships.

§ 12 Nouns – gender

All nouns are either masculine, feminine or neuter. If there is an article it is easy to recognize the gender.

Masculine	*Feminine*	*Neuter*
der Hund	**die** Katze	**das** Pferd
der Fluss	**die** Straße	**das** Haus
der Wein	**die** Cola	**das** Bier

You need to know what gender a noun is, otherwise you can't choose the correct forms of …

- … the article:
  der, **die** or **das**?
- … the personal pronoun:
  der Fluss ▶ **er** heißt Rhein,
  die Straße ▶ **sie** ist lang,
  das Haus ▶ **es** ist alt.
- … the possessive pronoun:
  die Katze ▶ **meine** Katze.
- … the adjective ending:
  der Hund ▶ ein braun**er** Hund.

Unfortunately, in most cases you cannot recognise the gender from the noun itself. So it's advisable that you always learn the definite article together with the noun.

However, there are some features like typical endings or word groups that help you to recognise the gender.

Masculine nouns

Features	*Examples*
-er	der Bäcker, der Lehrer
Seasons	der Frühling, der Sommer
Months	der Januar, der Februar
Days of the week	der Montag, der Dienstag
Directions	der Norden, der Süden

Feminine nouns

Features	*Examples*
-e	die Katze, die Blume *but:* **der** Name, **der** Kollege
-in	die Freundin, die Schülerin, die Bäckerin, die Lehrerin
-frau	die Geschäftsfrau
-ei	die Bäckerei, die Metzgerei
-ung	die Bestellung, die Verbindung
Foreign words in **-ät**, **-ik**, **-ion**, **-ie** and **-ur**	die Universität, die Musik, die Information, die Biologie, die Kultur

Neuter nouns

Features	*Examples*
-chen	das Brötchen, das Küsschen
-um	das Zentrum, das Museum
Colours	das Rot, das Blau
Countries	Deutschland, Österreich etc. *(used without article)* *but:* **die** Schweiz, **die** Türkei *(always used with the article)*

§ 13 Nouns – singular

The noun itself isn't declined in the singular. Only the article shows up the case and the gender of the noun.

	Masculine	*Feminine*	*Neuter*
Nom.	der Fluss	die Stadt	das Land
Acc.	den Fluss	die Stadt	das Land
Dat.	dem Fluss	der Stadt	dem Land

But: Masculine nouns in **-e** follow another declination (see § **Masculine nouns in *-e***):

	Masculine in ***-e***
Nom.	der Kollege
Acc.	den Kollege**n**
Dat.	dem Kollege**n**

§ 14 Nouns – plural

Declination

	Masculine	*Feminine*	*Neuter*
Nom.	die Flüsse	die Städte	die Länder
Acc.	die Flüsse	die Städte	die Länder
Dat.	den Flüsse**n**	den Städte**n**	den Länder**n**

Note: The dative plural always ends in **-n**.
Exception: Foreign words have the ending **-s**:
den Clown**s**, den Café**s**, den Foto**s** etc.

Masculine nouns ending in **-e** follow another declination pattern. See **§ Masculine nouns in *-e***.

Endings of the plural

Depending on the gender of the noun and their singular ending there are six different endings for the plural:

-e, **-n**, **-en**, **-er**, **-s** or no ending

If there's a vowel **a**, **o**, **u** in the noun, it is mostly changed to **ä**, **ö**, **ü**.

Here are the rules:

1. Masculine or neuter nouns in **-el**, **-en**, **-er** don't have any plural ending:

der Spiegel	die Spiegel
das Brötchen	die Brötchen
das Fenster	die Fenster

2. Other masculine or neuter nouns end in **-e**:

der Fluss	die Fl<u>ü</u>ss**e**
das Regal	die Regal**e**

3. Neuter nouns with one-syllable end in **-er**:

das Dorf	die D<u>ö</u>r**fer**
das Bild	die Bild**er**

4. Feminine nouns in **-e** end in **-n**:

die Banane	die Banane**n**
die Straße	die Straße**n**

5. Feminine nouns ending in consonant or another vowel than **-e** have the plural ending **-en**:

die Tür	die Tür**en**
die Frau	die Frau**en**
die Kollegin	die Kollegin<u>n</u>**en**

6. Foreign words (all gender) end in **-s**:

das Foto	die Foto**s**
die Party	die Party**s**

Exceptions:
Unfortunately, there are a lot of exceptions. Here are only some of the most common ones:

der Mann	die Männer
der Vater	die Väter
die Mutter	die Mütter
die Tochter	die Töchter

Irregular plural forms:

das Material	die Materialien
das Museum	die Museen
das Praktikum	die Praktika

§ 15 Word order

Basic word order patterns

Depending on the position of the verb there are two basic word order patterns: the normal and the inverted word order.

1. Normal word order

Verb = 2nd position

This structure is used for assertions and questions with interrogatives.

Assertions:

Subject	*Verb*	*Complements*
Herr Müller	**lebt**	in Deutschland.
Ich	**komme**	aus Köln.

If you put another word than the subject into the first position, the subject is placed behind the verb. Compare:
Ich **besuche** heute meine Tante.
I'm visiting my aunt today.
Heute **besuche** ich meine Tante.
Today I'm visiting my aunt.

After **und** *(and)*, **oder** *(or)* and **aber** *(but)* you always have the normal word order:
Sie mag Wein, aber er trinkt lieber Bier.
She likes wine, but he prefers drinking beer.

Questions with interrogatives:

Interrogative	*Verb*	*Subject*	*Complements*
Wo	**lebt**	Peter	jetzt?
Wann	**kommst**	du	nach Hause?

2. Inverted word order

Verb = 1st position

Yes/No- questions:
Yes/no- questions start with the verb followed by the subject.

Verb	*Subject*	*Complements*
Kommst	du	aus Italien?
Sind	Sie	Fotografin?

Imperative:

Verb	*Subject*	*Complements*
Kommen	Sie	bitte pünktlich!
Komm		bitte pünktlich!
Kommt		bitte pünktlich!

Note that only in the polite form of the imperative you'll encounter a subject.

Sentences with various complements

Apart from the word order patterns above that point out the position of the verb and the subject, we have to focus also on the complements.

Complements can be:	*Examples:*
Accusative objects:	Ich schreibe **einen Brief**.
Dative objects:	Ich schreibe **meiner Oma**.

Prepositional phrases	
of location:	Ich wohne **in Düsseldorf**.
of direction:	Ich fahre **nach Berlin**.
of origin:	Ich komme **aus Italien**.
of time:	Ich komme **am Sonntag**.

All these complements come behind the verb. When you combine them in one sentence watch out for the following word order rules.

Rules for dative and accusative objects

If you have got a dative and an accusative object in one sentence the dative comes first.

Dative – Accusative (noun)

Ich schreibe **meiner Oma** einen Brief.
I'm writing a letter to my grandma.

This rule is also valid if the dative object is a pronoun (**mir**, **dir**, **ihm**, **ihr** etc.).

Ich schreibe **ihr** einen Brief.
I'm writing a letter to her.

But: If you replace the accusative object with a pronoun (**mich**, **dich**, **ihn**, **sie** etc.) the word order changes.

Accusative (pronoun) – Dative

Ich schreibe **ihn** meiner Oma.
Ich schreibe **ihn** ihr.

Rules for prepositional phrases

In general, prepositional phrases are placed at the end of the sentence:

Dative / Accusative – Prepositional phrases

Ich schreibe ihr einen Brief **zum Geburtstag**.
I'm writing her a letter to her birthday.
Ich besuche meine Oma **in Berlin**.
I'm visiting my grandma in Berlin.

Prepositional phrase of time – Other prepositional phrase

If there are two or more prepositional phrases in one sentence and if one of them is an expression of time like **am Donnerstag** *(on Thursday)*, **um 10 Uhr** *(at 10 o'clock)*, **im Januar** *(in January)* etc. the prepositional phrase of time comes first.

Ich fahre am Donnerstag mit Peter nach Berlin.
I'll be going to Berlin on Thursday with Peter.
Wir heiraten am 23. August in München.
We're going to get married in Munich on 23rd August.

When looking at the word order rules, these references might also be interesting:
§ **Adverbs** informs you about the position of the adverb in the sentence.
§ **Modal verbs** informs you about the different positions of modal verbs in the sentence.
§ **Perfect tense** informs you about the word order within a present perfect sentence.
§ **Subordinate clauses** informs you about the word order within subordinate clauses.

§ 16 Past participle

You need the past participle to form the perfect tense (see **§ Perfect tense**).

Regular verbs

ge- unchanged present stem **-t**

lernen *(to learn)*	**ge**lern**t**
suchen *(to look for)*	**ge**such**t**
machen *(to make)*	**ge**mach**t**

Verbs in **-den** or **-ten** get the ending **-et**:

reden *(to talk)*	**ge**red**et**
arbeiten *(to work)*	**ge**arbeit**et**

Irregular verbs

ge- often a changed stem **-en**

kommen *(to come)*	**ge**komm**en**
gehen *(to go)*	**ge**gang**en**
treffen *(to meet)*	**ge**troff**en**
but:	
bringen *(to bring)*	**ge**brach**t** (!)
denken *(to think)*	**ge**dach**t** (!)

Verbs with separable prefixes
The most common separable prefixes are: **ab-**, **an-**, **auf-**, **aus-**, **ein-**, **hin-**, **los-**, **mit-**, **teil-**, **um-**, **vor-**, **weg-**, **weiter-** and **zurück-**.

Verbs with separable prefixes can be regular or irregular:

Prefix **-ge-** unchanged present stem **-t**

vorhaben *(to have planned)*	vor**ge**hab**t**
auspacken *(to unwrap)*	aus**ge**pack**t**

Prefix **-ge-** often a changed stem **-en**

einladen *(to invite)*	ein**ge**lad**en**
aussteigen *(to get off)*	aus**ge**stieg**en**

Verbs beginning with *be-*, *ent-*, *er-*, *ver-*
These verbs don't have the marker **-ge-** and can be regular or irregular:

unchanged present stem **-t**

erzählen *(to tell)*	erzähl**t**
bestellen *(to order)*	bestell**t**

often a changed stem **-en**

bekommen *(to get)*	bekomm**en**
verstehen *(to understand)*	verstand**en**

Verbs in *-ieren*
Verbs in **-ieren** are regular, but they don't have the marker **-ge-**:

unchanged present stem **-t**

studieren *(to study)*	studier**t**
probieren *(to try)*	probier**t**

If you aren't sure whether a verb is irregular or not look at the glossary.

§ 17 Past tense

Conjugation

	haben	sein
ich	ha**tt**e	**war**
du	ha**tt**est	**war**st
er/sie/es	ha**tt**e	**war**
wir	ha**tt**en	**war**en
ihr	ha**tt**et	**war**t
sie	ha**tt**en	**war**en
Polite form:		
Sie	ha**tt**en	**war**en

	können	wollen	müssen
ich	konn**t**e	woll**t**e	muss**t**e
du	konn**t**est	woll**t**est	muss**t**est
er/sie/es	konn**t**e	woll**t**e	muss**t**e
wir	konn**t**en	woll**t**en	muss**t**en
ihr	konn**t**et	woll**t**et	muss**t**et
sie	konn**t**en	woll**t**en	muss**t**en
Polite form:			
Sie	konn**t**en	woll**t**en	muss**t**en

The marker of the past tense is the **-t-** for the regular forms. The irregular verb **sein** has the past stem **war**.
The personal endings are the normal endings for the present tense. Exception: The 3rd person singular of the regular forms is given an **-e** and the forms **ich/er war** are irregular.

Use

Written language:
The past tense is used especially in the written language, when a story starts and ends in the past. A typical beginning of a fairy-tale is:

Es **war** einmal ein kleines Kind. Es **hatte** keine Eltern und **musste** …
Once upon a time there was a little child. It had no parents and had to …

Spoken language:
It is much more common to use the perfect tense when talking about the past (see **§ Perfect tense**). In the spoken language, only the past tense of a few verbs like **haben** and **sein** and the past of modals is really used.

Als Kind **wollte** ich Zahnärztin **werden**.
As a child I wanted to become a dentist.
Wir **mussten** gestern nach Wien **fahren**.
We had to go to Vienna yesterday.
Warum **konntest** du nicht **kommen**?
Why couldn't you come?
Hatten Sie 1964 schon ein Auto?
Did you already have a car in 1974?
Früher **war** ich oft allein.
I used to be alone a lot.

§ 18 Perfect tense

The perfect tense is the most important past tense in German. It's used in the spoken language, in conversations. Note that the use of the German perfect tense doesn't automatically correspond with the present perfect in English or the perfect tense in your native language.

The perfect tense is a compound tense consisting of two parts:

present tense of **haben** or **sein** + past participle of the verb

Conjugation

	lernen	**kommen**
ich	habe gelernt	bin gekommen
du	hast gelernt	bist gekommen
er/sie/es	hat gelernt	ist gekommen
wir	haben gelernt	sind gekommen
ihr	habt gelernt	seid gekommen
sie	haben gelernt	sind gekommen
Polite form:		
Sie	haben gelernt	sind gekommen

Rules about the participle forms are explained in the section **§ Past participle**.

Haben or sein?

Most verbs take **haben** to form the perfect tense. Reflexive verbs always take **haben**.

Sein is used for verbs that indicate …
(a) motion:

kommen *(to come)*	ich bin gekommen
gehen *(to go)*	ich bin gegangen
fahren *(to go, to drive)*	ich bin gefahren
schwimmen *(to swim)*	ich bin geschwommen

(b) a change of condition:

aufstehen *(to get up)*	ich bin aufgestanden
einsteigen *(to get on)*	ich bin eingestiegen

(c) an event:

geschehen *(to happen)*	es ist geschehen

(only the 3rd person singular is used)

Two exceptions:

sein *(to be)*	ich **bin** gewesen
bleiben *(to stay)*	ich **bin** geblieben

Word order

The conjugated verb **haben** or **sein** is in the usual verb position (second position in assertions and questions with interrogative pronouns, first position in yes/no-questions). The past participle is always placed at the very end of the sentence.

Er	**ist**	nicht	**gekommen.**
Ich	**habe**	dort Englisch	**gelernt.**
Wo	**bist**	du am Montag	**gewesen**?
	Sind	Sie nach Köln	**gefahren**?

§ 19 Personal pronouns

Forms

Singular	*Nom.*	*Acc.*	*Dat.*
1st p.	ich	mich	mir
2nd p. (familiar)	du	dich	dir
2nd p. (polite)	Sie	Sie	Ihnen
3rd persons	er	ihn	ihm
	sie	sie	ihr
	es	es	ihm

Plural	*Nom.*	*Acc.*	*Dat.*
1st p.	wir	uns	uns
2nd p. (familiar)	ihr	euch	euch
2nd p. (polite)	Sie	Sie	Ihnen
3rd p.	sie	sie	ihnen

The polite forms **Sie** *(you)* and **Ihnen** *(to you)* are capitalised.

Use

Subject and object

The personal pronouns are used ...

(a) ... as subject (nominative case):
Er lebt in Berlin.
He lives in Berlin.
Wir sind aus Wien, und **ihr**?
We are from Vienna, and you?
Sind **Sie** Frau Müller?
Are you Mrs. Müller?

(b) ... as direct object (accusative case):
Peter, hier ist ein Anruf für **dich.**
Peter, there is a phone call for you.
Ich kann **ihn** nicht sehen.
I can't see him.

(c) ... as indirect object (dative case):
Wie geht es **Ihnen**? Wie geht es **dir**?
How are you?
Können Sie **mir** bitte helfen?
Can you help me, please?

Special uses of *es*

The pronoun **es** is used as a formal subject in sentences about the weather and the time.

Es regnet.	*It's raining.*
Es ist 8 Uhr.	*It's 8 o'clock.*

The expression **es gibt** *(there is, there are)* is only used in the singular, even if the direct object is in the plural. Compare:

Es gibt nur einen Turm.
There is only one tower.
Es gibt nur zwei Türme.
There are only two towers.

§ 20 Possessive pronouns

Every time you talk about belongings you need possessive pronouns like **mein** *(my)*, **dein** *(your)* etc. Here are the possessive pronouns without endings:

Singular		
ich	**mein**	*my*
du	**dein**	*your (familiar)*
Sie	**Ihr**	*your (polite)*
er	**sein**	*his*
sie	**ihr**	*her*
es	**sein**	*its*

Plural		
wir	**unser**	*our*
ihr	**euer**	*your (familiar)*
Sie	**Ihr**	*your (polite)*
sie	**ihr**	*their*

Note that the polite form **Ihr** is capitalised.

Declination

Depending on gender, case and number of the noun the possessive pronouns are given the following endings:

Singular	*Masculine*	*Feminine*
Nom.	mein Hund	mein**e** Katze
Acc.	mein**en** Hund	mein**e** Katze
Dat.	mein**em** Hund	mein**er** Katze

Singular	*Neuter*	*Plural All Gender*
Nom.	mein Pferd	mein**e** Tiere
Acc.	mein Pferd	mein**e** Tiere
Dat.	mein**em** Pferd	mein**en** Tieren

The singular forms have the same endings as the indefinite article **ein** and the plural forms have the same endings as the negated indefinite article **kein.**

Kommt **dein** Bruder auch?
Is your brother coming, too?
Frau Müller, ist das **Ihre** Tasche?
Mrs. Müller, is this your bag?
Wir treffen uns mit **unseren** Kollegen am Freitag.
We are meeting our colleagues on Friday.

The declined forms of **euer** drop the second **e**:

Wo sind **eure** Eltern?
Where are your parents?

Use of sein and ihr

Watch out for the use in the 3rd person singular. **Sein** *(his)* refers to a male "owner" and **ihr** *(her)* to a female "owner". Compare:

Er besucht **seine** Eltern und **seinen** Bruder.
He's visiting his parents and his brother.
Sie besucht **ihre** Eltern und **ihren** Bruder.
She's visiting her parents and her brother.

§ 21 Prepositions

Prepositions are used without an article in front of proper names (exception: names of streets):

Ich fahre **zu** Peter / **nach** Bonn / **nach** Polen.
I'm going to Peter's / to Bonn / to Poland.

but:

Ich fahre **in die** Bäckerstraße.
I'm going to Baker Street.

With exception of proper names, prepositions are in general followed by an article, a possessive pronoun or demonstrative pronoun, which are declined in the case that the preposition governs.

Ich fahre **immer** mit de**m** Bus. (▸ dative)
I always go by bus.
Ich fahre nicht **ohne** mein**en** Freund. (▸ accusative)
I'm not going without my friend.

Prepositions with accusative

bis *(till, to)*, **durch** *(through)* **entlang** *(along)*, **für** *(for)*, **gegen** *(against, about)*, **ohne** *(without)*, **um** *(at)*

bis (zu)	Fahren Sie **bis** zur Bäckerstraße. *Go until you get to Baker street.* Tschüss! **Bis** Montag! *Bye-bye. Till Monday!*
durch	Ich gehe gern **durch** den Park. *I like walking through the park.*
entlang	Geh diese Straße **entlang.** *Go along this street.*
für	Ein Geschenk **für** Lisa. *A gift for Lisa.*
gegen	Das Auto ist **gegen** das Haus gefahren. *The car drove into the house.* Es ist **gegen** 4 Uhr. *It's about 4 o'clock.*
ohne	Eine Wohnung **ohne** Balkon. *A flat without a balcony.*
um	Der Zug kommt **um** 3 Uhr an. *The train arrives at 3 o'clock.*

Note: The preposition **entlang** is placed behind the noun.

Prepositions with dative

aus *(from, of)*, **bei** *(with, near, at)*, **gegenüber** *(opposite, across the road)*, **mit** *(with)*, **nach** *(after, to, past)*, **seit** *(since, for)*, **von** *(from, by, of)*, **zu** *(to)*

aus	Woher kommst du? – **Aus** Österreich. *Where are you from? – From Austria.* Der Tisch ist **aus** Holz. *The table is made of wood.*
bei	Er wohnt **bei** seinen Eltern. *He lives with his parents.* Wir treffen uns **bei** der Kirche. *We meet near the church.*
gegenüber	**Gegenüber** dem Kiosk ist die Post. *The post office is opposite the kiosk.*
mit	Einen Apfelkuchen **mit** Sahne, bitte. *An apple pie with whipped cream, please.*
nach	Morgen fahre ich **nach** Berlin. *Tomorrow I'm going to Berlin.* Wie spät ist es? – Es ist 10 **nach** 2. *What time is it? – It's 10 past 2.* Was machst du **nach** dem Frühstück? *What do you do after breakfast?*
seit	Ich bin **seit** 1998 verheiratet. *I'm married since 1998.*

▼

von Er kommt **vom** Arzt zurück.
He's coming back from the doctor.
Hast du einen Stadtplan **von** Bonn?
Do you have a map of Bonn?

zu Wie komme ich **zum** Bahnhof?
How do I get to the railway station?

The following prepositions are usually contracted with the definite article:

bei, von, zu + dem ▶ **beim**, **vom**, **zum**
zu + der ▶ **zur**

Prepositions with accusative and dative

an *(at, on, to)*, **auf** *(at, in, on)*, **hinter** *(behind)*, **in** *(in, into, to)*, **neben** *(beside, next to)*, **über** *(over)*, **unter** *(under)*, **vor** *(in front of)*, **zwischen** *(between)*

Rules and use

Wohin? (*Where to?*)	**Wo?** (*Where?*)
Direction, destination, motion	Position, location
Accusative	**Dative**
Wohin geht er? – Ins Bett. (*To bed.*)	Wo ist er? – Im Bett. (*In bed.*)

Compare the use of the accusative (A) and the dative (D) in the following examples:

an Er hängt das Bild **an die** Wand. (A)
He's hanging the picture on the wall.
Das Bild hängt **an der** Wand. (D)
The picture is (hanging) on the wall.

auf Er legt die Jacke **auf das** Sofa. (A)
He's putting the jacket on the sofa.
Die Jacke liegt **auf dem** Sofa. (D)
The jacket is (lying) on the sofa.

in Wir gehen **in den** Park. (A)
We go into the park.
Das Kind spielt **im** Park. (D)
The child is playing in the park.

über Häng die Lampe **über den** Tisch! (A)
Hang the lamp over the table!
Die Lampe hängt **über dem** Tisch. (D)
The lamp is hanging over the table.

vor Geht **vor das** Haus! (A)
Go in front of the house.
Vor dem Haus ist ein Garten. (D)
In front of the house there is a garden.

Note that the preposition **auf** (instead of **in**) is used with offices or institutions:

Ich gehe **auf die Bank.**
I'm going to the bank.
Er ist **auf der Post.**
He's at the post office.

The prepositions **an** and **in** have a temporal meaning, too. In this meaning they govern the dative case:

Wir heiraten **im** August.
We are getting married in August.
Am Freitag fahre ich nach Wien.
On Friday I'm going to Vienna.
Ich bin **am** 12. Juli 1974 geboren.
I was born on 12th July 1974.
Meine Tante kommt **am** Nachmittag.
My aunt is coming in the afternoon.

but:

Ich bin 1974 geboren. (without preposition!)
I was born in 1974.

The following prepositions are usually contracted with the definite article:

in, an + dem ▶ **im**, **am**
in, an, auf +das ▶ **ins**, **ans**, **aufs**

§ 22 Present tense

Regular verbs

	wohnen		**arbeiten**	**heißen**
ich	wohne	**-e**	arbeite	heiße
du	wohnst	**-st**	arbeitest	hei**ßt**
er/sie/es	wohnt	**-t**	arbeitet	heißt
wir	wohnen	**-en**	arbeiten	heißen
ihr	wohnt	**-t**	arbeitet	heißt
sie	wohnen	**-en**	arbeiten	heißen
Polite form:				
Sie	wohnen	**-en**	arbeiten	heißen

▼

The present tense of most German verbs is formed by dropping the infinitive ending **-en** and adding a personal ending to the stem (**wohn-**, **arbeit-**, **heiß-**).

If the stem ends in **-d** or **-t** (**baden**, **arbeiten**) you insert an **e** between stem and ending.

Lisa bad**e**t gern.
Lisa likes having a bath.
Arbeit**e**t ihr morgen?
Are you working tomorrow?

If the stem ends in **-s**, **-ß** or **-z**, the 2nd person singular gets the ending **-t**.

Du tan**zt** sehr gut. – *You dance very well.*
Wie hei**ßt** du? – *What's your name?*

Verbs with stem-vowel changes

A number of verbs change the stem-vowel, but luckily only in the 2nd and 3rd person singular.

e ▸ i ("short **i**")

sprechen:	ich spreche, du spr**i**chst, er spr**i**cht
geben:	ich gebe, du g**i**bst, er g**i**bt
essen:	ich esse, du **i**sst, er **i**sst
treffen:	ich treffe, du tr**i**ffst, er tr**i**fft
helfen:	ich helfe, du h**i**lfst, er h**i**lft
nehmen:	ich nehme, du n**i**mmst, er n**i**mmt (!)

e ▸ ie ("long **i**")

sehen:	ich sehe, du s**ie**hst, er s**ie**ht
lesen:	ich lese, du l**ie**st, er l**ie**st

a ▸ ä

fahren:	ich fahre, du f**ä**hrst, er f**ä**hrt
schlafen:	ich schlafe, du schl**ä**fst, er schl**ä**ft
halten:	ich halte, du h**ä**ltst, er h**ä**lt

Note that not all verbs with **e** or **a** change the stem-vowel. In the glossary you can find the paradigm of the verbs which change the stem-vowel.

Irregular verbs

Some of the most frequently used verbs are irregular, e.g. **sein** *(to be)*, **haben** *(to have)*, **werden** *(to become)* and **wissen** *(to know)*:

	sein	haben	werden	wissen
ich	bin	habe	werde	weiß
du	bist	hast	wirst	weißt
er/sie/es	ist	hat	wird	weiß
wir	sind	haben	werden	wissen
ihr	seid	habt	werdet	wisst
sie	sind	haben	werden	wissen
Polite form:				
Sie	sind	haben	werden	wissen

Use of the present tense

The present tense has a very broad usage. You can use it …

(a) for a temporary situation:
Ich **gehe** jetzt ins Bett. Gute Nacht!
I'm going to bed now. Goodnight!

(b) for a permanent situation and event:
Meine Eltern **leben** in München.
My parents live in Munich.

(c) for a situation in the future:
Peter **kommt** morgen.
Peter will be arriving tomorrow.

§ 23 Reflexive verbs

A verb is called reflexive because the reflexive pronoun refers back to the subject and is identical with it.
The marker for the infinitive of a reflexive verb is the pronoun **sich** *(oneself)*.

Present tense

	sich interessieren	
ich	interessiere	mich
du	interessierst	dich
er/sie/es	interessiert	sich
wir	interessieren	uns
ihr	interessiert	euch
sie	interessieren	sich
Polite form:		
Sie	interessieren	sich

▼

Use and word order

In assertions and questions with an interrogative, the reflexive pronoun is placed behind the verb, in yes/no-questions it is placed behind the subject.

Ich interessiere mich für Kunst.
I'm interested in art.
Das Wetter ändert sich.
The weather is changing.
Freust du dich auf die Party?
Are you looking forward to the party?

Many German verbs can be reflexive and not reflexive:

sich anziehen	Ich ziehe mich an. *I'm getting dressed.*
anziehen	Ich ziehe die Jacke an. *I'm putting on the jacket.*

Perfect tense

The perfect tense of reflexive verbs is always formed by the auxiliary verb **haben**:

ich habe mich geändert
du hast dich gefreut
er hat sich angezogen etc.

§ 24 Separable verbs

In German, there are a lot of verbs with a separable prefix. The infinitive of a separable verb like **ankommen** *(to arrive)* is written as one word. But to form a correct sentence in the present tense and in the imperative, the prefix **an-** must be removed and placed at the very end of the sentence.

ankommen:	Wir **kommen** um 8 Uhr **an**. *We're arriving at 8 o'clock.*
abfahren:	Um wie viel Uhr **fährt** der Zug **ab**? *At what time does the train leave?*
vorbereiten:	Susanne **bereitet** das Picknick **vor**. *Susanne is preparing the picnic.*
wegwerfen:	**Wirf** die Tüte nicht **weg**! *Don't throw the bag away!*

About the separable prefix

The separable prefix is always stressed:
abfahren, ich fahre **ab**.

The most common separable prefixes are: **ab-**, **an-**, **auf-**, **aus-**, **ein-**, **hin-**, **los-**, **mit-**, **teil-**, **um-**, **vor-**, **weg-**, **weiter-** and **zurück-**. Examples:

abfahren *(to leave)*, anrufen *(to call)*, aufstehen *(to get up)*, ausgehen *(to go out)*, einsteigen *(to get on)*, hinfahren *(to go there)*, losgehen *(to set off)*, mitnehmen *(to bring along)*, teilnehmen *(to take part)*, umsteigen *(to change)*, vorhaben *(to have planned)*, wegwerfen *(to throw away)*, weitergehen *(to go on)*, zurückgehen *(to go back)*

Don't forget that these little prefixes change the meaning of a verb. Compare:

kommen	*to come*
ankommen	*to arrive*
mitkommen	*to go along*
zurückkommen	*to return*

Prefix and verb reunited

Watch out for the writing of the verb with a separable prefix in the following cases:

Sentences with modals:
The verb with a separable prefix is written together because it occurs in the infinitive form:
Meine Frau kann nicht **mitkommen**.
My wife can't come along.

Perfect tense:
The **ge-** of the past participle is inserted between the prefix and the stem of the verb.
Wir sind gestern **angekommen**.
We arrived yesterday.

Subordinate clauses:
The prefix and the verb are reunited.
Ich denke, dass er nicht **teilnimmt**.
I think he won't take part.

§ 25 Subordinate clauses

In German, subordinate clauses have two markers:
1. they are introduced by a conjunction,
2. the word order changes.

Note that there is a comma between the main clause and the subordinate clause:

You already know the conjunctions:

wenn	1. *if, in case*, 2. *when*
dass	*that*
weil	*because*

The conjunctions

wenn
The conjunction **wenn** introduces a subordinate clause with a conditional *(if, in case)* or a temporal meaning *(when)*:

Wir gehen spazieren, **wenn** das Wetter schön ist.
We'll go for a walk if the weather is fine.
Er liest die Zeitung, **wenn** er frühstückt.
He reads the newspaper when he has breakfast.

weil
In order to give a reason for something you use a subordinate clause introduced by **weil** *(because)*.

Ich kann nicht mitkommen, **weil** ich arbeiten muss.
I cannot come along because I have to work.

To answer a question beginning with **warum?** *(why?)* you can use a **weil**-clause without the main clause.

Warum fährst du nicht mit dem Auto?
– **Weil** ich lieber zu Fuß gehe.
Why don't you go by car?
– Because I prefer walking.

dass
The conjunction **dass** *(that)* is used to report a thought, a speech, a supposition or an opinion etc. of yourself or of somebody else. The exact function depends on the meaning of the verb of the main clause, e.g.:

Ich vermute, **dass** er bald kommt. *(Supposition)*
I suppose he'll be arriving soon.
Ich denke, **dass** du Recht hast. *(Opinion)*
I think you are right.
Sie hat mir erzählt, **dass** sie einen neuen Freund hat. *(Reported speech)*
She told me that she has a new boyfriend.

Word order

The conjugated verb is always at the end of the subordinate clause. Verbs with separable prefixes are reunited.
Compare the word order of the main clause and the corresponding subordinate clause in the following examples:

Ich habe keine Zeit.
Ich komme nicht mit, weil ich keine Zeit **habe.**
I'm not coming along because I don't have any time.

Er kommt um 3 Uhr an.
Er sagt, dass er um 3 Uhr **ankommt.**
He says that he'll be arriving at 3 o'clock.

Er muss nicht arbeiten.
Er freut sich, wenn er nicht **arbeiten muss.**
He's glad when he doesn't have to work.

§ 26 Verbs with prepositions

Many verbs are followed by a preposition plus an accusative (A) or dative (D) and they have to be learnt by heart:

einladen zu + D	*to invite to*
halten von + D	*to think of*
sich bedanken für + A	*to thank for*
sich freuen auf + A	*to look forward to*
sich freuen über + A	*to be pleased about*
sich interessieren für + A	*to be interested in*
sich treffen mit + D	*to meet*
teilnehmen an + D	*to take part in*
warten auf + A	*to wait for*

A

der	Abend	*evening*
das	Abendessen	*dinner*
	aber	*but*
	abgeben	*give sb sth*
	abholen	*pick up*
	ablehnen	*disapprove*
	absagen	*decline*
	abwaschen	*wash up*
	ach nein	*oh no*
	ach was!	*come on!*
	ah!	*ah!, oh!*
	aha	*I see*
der	Alkohol	*alcohol*
	alles	*all*
	alles Gute	*all the best*
	als	*as*
	alt	*old*
	am	*see preposition an*
die	Ampel	*traffic light*
sich	amüsieren	*amuse oneself*
	an	*at*
	anbieten	*offer*
	andere(r)	*other*
	anders	*different*
	anfangen	*start*
	anhaben	*wear*
	anrufen	*call, phone*
	ansehen	*look at*
	antworten	*answer*
	anziehen	*put on*
sich	anziehen	*get dressed*
der	Anzug	*suit*
die	Apotheke	*chemist's*
die	Apothekerin	*chemist*
die	Arbeit	*work*
	arbeiten	*work*
	arm	*poor*
der	Arzt	*doctor*
	atmen	*breathe*
	auch	*also, too*
	auf	*for*
	aufessen	*eat up*
	aufhören	*stop, quit*
	aufmachen	*open*
	aufräumen	*tidy up*
	aus	*from*
der	Ausflug	*outing*
	ausgeben	*spend*
	ausgezeichnet	*excellent*
	ausmachen	*switch off*
	ausruhen	*rest*
	aussehen	*look (like)*
	Australien	*Australia*
	austrinken	*drink up*
das	Auto	*car*

B

der	Bäcker	*baker*
die	Bäckerei	*baker's*
der	Bahnhof	*railway station*
die	Band	*band*
der	Bauer	*farmer*
die	Baumwolle	*cotton*
sich	bedanken	*thank*
	beeilen	*hurry*
	beginnen	*begin*
	begrüßen	*greet/welcome*
	bei	*by*
	beide	*both*
das	Bein	*leg*
	bequem	*comfortable*
	beraten	*advise*
der	Beruf	*profession*
	berühmt	*famous*
sich	beschäftigen	*keep oneself busy*
	besonders	*especially*
	bestellen	*order*
	bestimmt	*certainly*
	besuchen	*visit*
	bezahlen	*pay*
das	Bier	*beer*
	bis	*until/till*
	Bis dann!	*See you*
	bitte	*please*
	bleiben	*stay*
die	Blume	*flower*
das	Blumengeschäft	*flower shop*
die	Bohne	*bean*
das	Boot	*boat*
	braten	*fry*
die	Bratwurst	*frying sausage*

der	Brief	*letter*
	bringen	*bring*
das	Brot	*bread*
der	Bruder	*brother*
das	Buch	*book*
	buchen	*book*
der	Buchstabe	*letter*
der	Bürgermeister	*mayor*
das	Büro	*office*
der	Bürostuhl	*office chair*

C

das	Café	*café*
die	CD (Compact Disk)	*CD*
der	Champagner	*champagne*
der	Chef	*boss*
die	Cola	*coke*
der	Computer	*computer*
der	Computertisch	*computer table*

D

	danach	*after that*
	danke	*thank you*
	danken	*thank*
	dann	*then*
	das	*the*
	Das ist schade!	*It's a pity!*
	dass	*that*
	dazu	*with it*
	definitiv	*definite*
	dein(e)	*your*
	den	*this*
	denken	*think*
	deutsch	*German*
der	Deutsche	*German*
	Deutschland	*Germany*
	dick	*fat*
	die	*the*
	dir	*you*
die	Disco	*disco*
	doch	*normally not translated*
	dreimal	*three times*
	du	*you*
	dunkel	*dark*
	dünn	*thin*
	durch	*through*
der	Durchschnitt	*average*
	dürfen	*be allowed to, may*
	duschen	*have a shower*

E

die	Ecke	*corner*
das	Ei	*egg*
	ein paar	*a few*
	ein(e)	*a*
	einfach	*simply*
	einkaufen	*do the shopping*
das	Einkaufszentrum	*shopping mall*
	einladen	*invite*
die	Einladung	*invitation*
	einpacken	*pack up*
	empfehlen	*recommend*
	England	*England*
der	Englischkurs	*English course*
der	Englischunterricht	*English classes*
	entlang	*along*
	entschließen	*decide to*
sich	entschuldigen	*excuse*
	er	*he*
	erklären	*explain*
	erst	*only*
der	Erwachsene	*adult*
	es	*it*
	es gibt	*there is, there are*
das	Essen	*food*
	essen	*eat*
	etwas	*a bit/something*
	euch	*you*
	euer/eure	*your*

F

	fahren	*go*
das	Fahrrad	*bicycle*
die	Familie	*family*
die	Farbe	*colour*
	fast	*nearly*
	fast so … wie	*almost as … as*
	feiern	*celebrate*
das	Fenster	*window*
	fernsehen	*watch TV*

	fertig	*ready*
das	Fett	*grease*
der	Film	*movie*
	finden	*find / think*
die	Firma	*company*
der	Fisch	*fish*
die	Flasche	*bottle*
das	Fleisch	*meat*
	fleißig	*hard-working*
	fliegen	*fly*
	flirten	*flirt*
das	Flugticket	*plane ticket*
das	Flugzeug	*airplane*
das	Foto	*photograph*
	fotografieren	*take a picture*
das	Fotomodel	*photographic model*
	Frankreich	*France*
die	Frau	*wife / woman*
der	Frauenabend	*girl's night*
	frei	*free*
sich	freuen	*be pleased / look forward to*
der	Freund	*friend*
der	Frisör	*hairdresser*
	früher	*in the past*
	frühstücken	*have breakfast*
	für	*for*
die	Fußgängerzone	*pedestrian precinct*

G

	ganz	*quite*
der	Garten	*garden*
der	Gast	*guest*
	geben	*give*
der	Geburtstag	*birthday*
das	Geburtstagslied	*birthday song*
das	Gedächtnis	*memory*
	gefallen	*like*
das	Gefühl	*feeling*
	gegen	*against*
	gegenüber	*opposite*
	gehen	*go*
das	Gelb	*yellow*
das	Geld	*money*
das	Gemüse	*vegetable*
	genauso ... wie	*as ... as*
	genießen	*enjoy*
	gerade	*at the moment*
	gern(e)	*with pleasure*
das	Geschäft	*shop*
das	Geschenk	*present*
das	Geschirr	*crockery*
	gießen	*water*
die	Gitarre	*guitar*
das	Glas	*glass*
	glauben	*believe*
	gleich	*at once*
	glücklich	*happy*
das	Golf	*golf*
	gratulieren	*congratulate*
	groß	*tall*
	grün	*green*
	gut	*good*
	Gute Besserung!	*Get well soon!*
	Guten Appetit!	*Enjoy your meal!*
	Guten Tag!	*good morning / good afternoon / hello*

H

	haben	*have*
	halten	*stop / hold*
	hängen	*hang*
	hart	*hard*
	hässlich	*ugly*
das	Haus	*house*
die	Hausfrau	*housewife*
die	Haustür	*front door*
	heiraten	*marry*
	heiß	*hot*
	heißen	*be called*
	helfen	*help*
	hell	*light*
das	Hemd	*shirt*
	herein kommen	*come in*
der	Herr	*Mister*
	heute	*today*
	hier	*here*
	Hier entlang!	*This way!*
die	Hilfe	*help*
	hinter	*behind*
	hoch	*high*
	hoffen	*hope*

	hoffentlich	*hopefully*
	höflich	*polite*
	Hör mal,	*Listen,*
	hören	*hear, listen*
der	Horrorfilm	*horror movie*
die	Hose	*trousers*
das	Hotel	*hotel*
der	Hunger	*hunger*
	Hunger haben	*be hungry*

I

	ich	*I*
die	Idee	*idea*
	ihm	*him*
	ihn	*him*
	Ihnen	*you*
	ihr	*you / her / their*
	Ihr	*your*
	im	*in*
	immer	*always*
	in	*in*
	ins	*see preposition in*
sich	interessieren	*be interested*
	irgendwie	*somehow*
	Italien	*Italy*
der	Italiener	*Italian restaurant*

J

	ja	*yes*
die	Jacke	*jacket*
	jawohl	*yes*
	jede(r)	*every*
	jetzt	*now*
	jung	*young*
der	Junge	*boy*

K

der	Kaffee	*coffee*
die	Kaffeemaschine	*coffee machine*
	kalt	*cold*
die	Kartoffel	*potato*
der	Kartoffelsalat	*potato salad*
der	Käse	*cheese*
die	Kassiererin	*cashier*
der	Katalog	*catalogue*
die	Katze	*cat*
	kaufen	*buy*
	kein Problem	*no problem*
	kein(e)	*no, any*
	Keine Sorge!	*Don't worry!*
der	Kellner	*waiter*
	kennen	*know*
das	Kind	*child*
die	Kinderärztin	*paediatrician*
das	Kino	*cinema, movie*
die	Kirche	*church*
der	Kirschkuchen	*cherry cake*
	klasse	*great*
das	Klavier	*piano*
das	Kleid	*dress*
die	Kleidung	*clothes*
	klein	*small*
	kochen	*boil / cook*
der	Koffer	*suitcase*
die	Kollegin	*colleague*
	kommen	*come*
	können	*can / be able to*
	krank	*ill*
das	Krankenhaus	*hospital*
die	Küche	*kitchen*
der	Kuchen	*cake*
der	Kuli	*ballpoint pen*
die	Kunst	*art*
die	Kunstausstellung	*art exhibition*
	kurz	*short*

L

	lächeln	*smile*
die	Lampe	*lamp*
	lang	*long*
	langweilen	*be bored*
	laufen	*walk / run*
die	Laune	*mood*
das	Leben	*life*
	lecker	*yummy / delicious*
die	Lehrerin	*teacher*
	Leid tun	*be sorry*
	leider	*unfortunately*
	lernen	*learn*
	lesen	*read*
die	Leute	*people*
	liebe(r)	*dear / beloved*

	lieben	*love*
	lieber	*rather*
die	Lieblingspizza	*favourite pizza*
	liegen	*lie somewhere*
	literweise	*by the litre*
	London	*London*
	los müssen	*have to leave*
	losgehen	*set off*
	lügen	*lie*
	lustig	*funny*

M

	machen	*make / do*
das	Mädchen	*girl*
	mal	*often not translated*
	malen	*paint*
die	Mama	*mum*
	man	*they, one, you*
	manchmal	*sometimes*
der	Mann	*man / husband*
das	Meer	*sea*
das	Mehl	*flour*
	mehr	*more*
	mein(e)	*my*
der	Mensch	*person*
der	Metzger	*butcher*
die	Metzgerei	*butcher's*
	Mexiko	*Mexico*
	mich	*me*
die	Milch	*milk*
die	Minute	*minute*
	mir	*me*
	mit	*with*
der	Mitarbeiter	*member of staff*
	mitbringen	*bring along*
	mitkommen	*come along*
	mitnehmen	*take along*
das	Model	*model*
die	Modenschau	*fashion show*
	modern	*fashionable*
	mögen	*like*
der	Moment	*moment*
	Moment mal!	*Hang on!*
der	Monat	*month*
der	Montag	*Monday*
der	Morgen	*morning*
	morgen	*tomorrow*
das	Museum	*museum*
die	Musik	*music*
	müssen	*must*
die	Mutter	*mother*

N

	Na dann!	*Well!*
	na ja	*well*
	nach	*to / for*
der	Nachbar	*neighbour*
	nachdenken	*think about sth*
	nachfragen	*ask, inquire*
die	Nachrichten	*news*
	nah	*near*
der	Name	*name*
	natürlich	*of course*
	neben	*near, beside, next to*
	nebenan	*next door*
	nehmen	*take*
	nein	*no*
	nett	*nice*
	neu	*new*
	nicht	*not*
	nicht wahr?	*don't you?*
	nichts	*nothing*
	nie	*never*
	noch	*still*
	noch etwas?	*anything else?*
	normal	*normal*
	nötig	*necessary*
die	Nudeln	*pasta*
die	Nummer	*number*
	nur	*only*

O

	oder	*or*
	oft	*often*
	oh ja	*oh yes*
	ohne	*without*
die	Oma	*grandmother*
der	Orangensaft	*orange juice*
	Österreich	*Austria*

P

	packen	*pack*
der	Papa	*dad*
das	Papier	*paper*
der	Park	*park*
der	Parkplatz	*car park*
die	Party	*party*
der	Pass	*passport*
die	Pfanne	*frying pan*
der	Pfarrer	*priest*
die	Pflanze	*plant*
das	Picknick	*picnic*
	picknicken	*picnic*
der	Picknickkorb	*picnic basket*
die	Pizza	*pizza*
die	Polizei	*police*
die	Postkarte	*postcard*
	praktisch	*practical*
die	Praxis	*surgery*
der	Preis	*price*
der	Pullover	*jumper*
	pünktlich	*on time*
	putzen	*clean*

R

	Rad fahren	*ride a bike*
	rasieren	*shave*
das	Rathaus	*town hall*
	rauchen	*smoke*
der	Redakteur	*editor*
die	Rede	*speech*
	reden	*talk*
das	Regal	*shelf*
die	Regel	*rule*
die	Reise	*journey*
das	Reisebüro	*travel agency*
der	Reiseführer	*guide book*
	reisen	*travel*
	rennen	*run*
das	Restaurant	*restaurant*
	richtig	*right*
der	Rock	*skirt*
das	Rot	*red*
	rot	*red*
	rufen	*call*

S

der	Saal	*hall*
die	Sachen	*things*
	sagen	*say*
der	Salat	*salad*
das	Salz	*salt*
der	Samstag	*Saturday*
	scharf	*spicy*
der	Schatz	*sweetheart*
	schenken	*give sb sth as a present*
	schlecht	*bad*
	schließen	*close*
der	Schlüssel	*key*
	schmecken	*taste*
	schneiden	*cut/slice*
	schnell	*quick*
die	Schokolade	*chocolate*
	schon	*already*
	schön	*pretty*
	schreiben	*write*
die	Schuhe	*shoes*
die	Schule	*school*
	schwimmen	*swim*
	sehen	*see*
	sehr	*very*
	Seht mal!	*Look!*
	sein	*be*
	sein(e)	*his, its*
	seit	*since, for*
die	Sekretärin	*secretary*
	selten	*seldom*
	sich	*oneself*
	sie	*she/they*
	Sie	*you*
	sieben	*seven*
	singen	*sing*
	sitzen	*sit*
	so	*so*
	so ... wie	*as ... as*
	so viel	*so much/many*
	sollen	*should, shall, be supposed to*
	sondern	*but*
die	Sonnencreme	*suncream*
der	Sonntag	*Sunday*

	sonst	*else*
das	Souvenir	*souvenir*
	sowieso	*anyway*
die	Spaghetti	*spaghetti*
	Spanien	*Spain*
	spät	*late*
	spazieren gehen	*go for a walk*
die	Speisekarte	*menu*
	spielen	*play*
der	Spitzensportler	*top sportsperson*
der	Sportler	*sportsman*
die	Sprache	*language*
	sprechen	*speak*
der	Staat	*state*
die	Stadt	*city/town*
der	Stadtplan	*street map*
der	Stadtteil	*district*
der	Star	*star (famous person)*
	startklar	*ready to go*
	stecken	*put into*
	stehen	*stand*
der	Strand	*beach*
die	Straße	*street/road*
der	Straßenname	*street name*
der	Stress	*stress*
die	Strümpfe	*socks*
der	Student	*student*
	studieren	*study*
der	Stuhl	*chair*
die	Stunde	*hour*
	suchen	*look for*
	super	*super, great*
der	Supermarkt	*supermarket*
die	Suppe	*soup*
der/die	Süße	*sweetie*

T

der	Tag	*day*
	täglich	*daily*
der	Tango	*tango*
	tanzen	*dance*
die	Tasche	*bag*
die	Tasse	*cup*
das	Taxi	*taxi*
der	Tee	*tea*
das	Telefon	*phone*
das	Telefonbuch	*phone book*
	telefonieren	*phone/call*
die	Telefonnummer	*phone number*
der	Tequila	*tequila*
	teuer	*expensive*
das	Ticket	*ticket*
der	Tierarzt	*vet*
der	Tisch	*table*
die	Tochter	*daughter*
	toll	*great*
	total	*totally*
der	Tourist	*tourist*
	tragen	*wear/carry*
	trainieren	*train*
der	Traum	*dream*
	treffen	*meet*
	trinken	*drink*
	tschüss	*bye*
das	T-Shirt	*T-shirt*
die	Tür	*door*

U

	über	*about/over*
	Uhr	*o'clock*
	um	*at/around*
	umrühren	*stir*
	und	*and*
die	Universität	*university*
	uns	*us*
	unser(e)	*our*
	unter	*under*
der	Urlaub	*holiday*

V

das	Vanilleeis	*vanilla ice-cream*
der	Vater	*father*
sich	verabreden	*arrange to meet*
	verbringen	*spend*
	vergessen	*forget*
die	Verkäuferin	*shop assistant*
	vermeiden	*avoid*
	vermuten	*suppose*
	verpassen	*miss*
	verrückt	*crazy*
sich	verspäten	*be late*

	verwechseln	*mix up sth*
	viel	*many*
	vielleicht	*perhaps/maybe*
die	Volkshochschule	*adult education centre*
das	Volleyball	*volleyball*
	von	*of*
	vor	*in front of*
	vorbereiten	*prepare*
	vorschlagen	*suggest*

W

	wahr	*true*
	wann	*when*
	warten	*wait*
	warum	*why*
	was	*what*
das	Wasser	*mineral water*
	wegfahren	*go away*
	weglassen	*leave out*
	weil	*because*
der	Wein	*wine*
	wem	*whom*
	wen	*whom*
	wenn	*when/if*
	wer	*who*
	werden	*become*
das	Wetter	*weather*
	wie	*how*
	wie viel(e)	*how much, what*
	wir	*we*
	wirklich	*really*
	wissen	*know*
	wo	*where*
die	Woche	*week*
das	Wochenende	*weekend*
	woher	*where from, how*
	wohin	*where … to*
	wohnen	*live*
die	Wohnung	*flat*
das	Wohnzimmer	*living room*
	wollen	*want*
das	Wort	*word*
	wünschen	*wish*
das	Würstchen	*little sausage*
	würzen	*season*

Z

der	Zahn	*tooth*
	zeigen	*show*
die	Zeit	*time*
die	Zeitung	*newspaper*
der	Zettel	*piece of paper*
das	Zimmer	*room*
	zu	*to/too*
	zu Fuß gehen	*walk*
	zu Hause	*at home*
der	Zucker	*sugar*
	zuerst	*at first*
	zum	*to*
	zumachen	*close*
	zunehmen	*gain weight*
	zurückrufen	*call back*
	zwanzig	*twenty*
	zwei	*two*
die	Zwiebel	*onion*
	zwischen	*between*

Recordings, sound editing and mastering:
Ton in Ton Medienhaus, Stuttgart

Sound editing:
ARTist Tonstudios, Pfullingen

Speakers:
Dorothea Baltzer
Gillian Bathmaker
Mark Borrill
Rudolf Guckelsberger
Lara Roßwag
Inge Spaughton
Michael Speer
Luise Wunderlich

Module 1
Track 1 – Übung 1
Track 2 – Übung 3
Track 3 – Übung 4
Track 4 – Übung 6
Track 5 – Übung 7
Track 6 – Übung 15

Test 1
Track 7 – Übung 3

Module 2
Track 8 – Übung 1
Track 9 – Übung 2
Track 10 – Übung 3
Track 11 – Übung 8
Track 12 – Übung 10
Track 13 – Übung 12

Module 3
Track 14 – Übung 1
Track 15 – Übung 6
Track 16 – Übung 12
Track 17 – Übung 15
Track 18 – Übung 16

Module 4
Track 19 – Übung 1
Track 20 – Übung 3
Track 21 – Übung 4
Track 22 – Übung 5
Track 23 – Übung 7
Track 24 – Übung 8
Track 25 – Übung 9
Track 26 – Übung 14

Module 5
Track 27 – Übung 1
Track 28 – Übung 3
Track 29 – Übung 7
Track 30 – Übung 9
Track 31 – Übung 12

Test 5
Track 32 – Übung 5

Module 6
Track 33 – Übung 1
Track 34 – Übung 3
Track 35 – Übung 5
Track 36 – Übung 6
Track 37 – Übung 10
Track 38 – Übung 13

Module 7
Track 39 – Übung 1
Track 40 – Übung 3
Track 41 – Übung 4
Track 42 – Übung 6
Track 43 – Übung 8
Track 44 – Übung 9
Track 45 – Übung 14
Track 46 – Übung 17

Test 7
Track 47 – Übung 4

Module 8
Track 48 – Übung 1
Track 49 – Übung 3
Track 50 – Übung 4
Track 51 – Übung 5
Track 52 – Übung 7
Track 53 – Übung 10
Track 54 – Übung 13

Module 9
Track 55 – Übung 1
Track 56 – Übung 4
Track 57 – Übung 8
Track 58 – Übung 10
Track 59 – Übung 12
Track 60 – Übung 13
Track 61 – Übung 14

Module 10
Track 62 – Übung 1
Track 63 – Übung 2
Track 64 – Übung 3
Track 65 – Übung 4
Track 66 – Übung 6
Track 67 – Übung 17

Test 10
Track 68 – Übung 3

Module 11
Track 69 – Übung 1
Track 70 – Übung 2
Track 71 – Übung 3
Track 72 – Übung 4
Track 73 – Übung 5
Track 74 – Übung 6
Track 75 – Übung 7
Track 76 – Übung 10
Track 77 – Übung 14

Test 11
Track 78 – Übung 3

Module 12
Track 79 – Übung 1
Track 80 – Übung 3
Track 81 – Übung 6
Track 82 – Übung 8
Track 83 – Übung 10
Track 84 – Übung 11
Track 85 – Übung 12

Notizen

Notizen

Notizen

Notizen

Notizen

Notizen

Notizen

Notizen

Notizen

Notizen

Notizen

Notizen

Notizen